THE DAILY WARRIOR

365 HOME WORKOUTS AND MEDITATIONS FOR TAKING ACTION, DEVELOPING STRENGTH, AND MAINTAINING DISCIPLINE

Heidi Leatherby

STARBOARD
TACTICAL

CONTENTS

Dedication 1

Introduction 2

How this Book Came to Be...2

How To Use This Book..4

Warming up, Stretching, and Cool downs 7

The Training Sessions 8

Common Concerns and Common Sense Advice 375

Glossary of Terms..382

About the Author 392

Notes 393

DEDICATION

To all of the coaches, mentors, athletes, and warriors who came before us. We truly stand on the shoulders of giants, many of whom are quoted in the pages to follow.

A special thank you to Tyson Bradley and John Murie of Altitude Athletics, Bozeman Montana.

Without you, none of this would have ever started. None of the training sessions to follow would have been written on the whiteboard day after day, year after year. Without your guidance, none of the hard work would have been endured, none of the accomplishments would have been experienced, and none of the strength and comradery would have been built.

You truly created a group of warriors during those countless hours of hard work, and many of those warriors continue to grow and teach to this day.

Thank you.

INTRODUCTION

How this Book Came to Be

I would like to express heartfelt gratitude to you for being open to explore the powerful impact of a daily practice of mental and physical strength.

Since the fall of 2013, I have systematically hand recorded each and every training session I've done, both in the gym and on my own. Sessions at the gym were completed at a place called Altitude Athletics in Bozeman Montana, under the supervision of two world class coaches and mentors, along with other visiting coaches from all over the country. Each day, a training session was written on an old whiteboard for all to follow, and I kept meticulous records of each one that we did.

Using this database of training sessions scribbled into Moleskine notebooks over the years, I've compiled what you will find in these pages referred to as the *Original Sessions*. Although most of the logged training sessions were accomplished using heavy equipment such as barbells, kettlebells, weight plates, pull-up bars, rings, and ropes, I've been able to modify everything in a way that is consumable and executed at home, with room for weights and equipment if you choose. These modified training sessions are based on the originals as much as possible, listed below each original session, and referred to as the *Home Editions*.

By no means do these versions of the originals make any of this easy, so it is your responsibility to ensure you are modifying accordingly.

Lastly, but certainly most importantly, I have included strength themed quotes at the start of each training session, to be used as a meditation as you are going through your training and your day. Use these as a way to train your mental attitude alongside your physical body. Without this piece, physical training will not be sustainable or nearly as effective.

It is my hope that you will be able to apply not only the physical training ideas here, but also practice mentally the quotes and meditations that go along with each, perhaps using this collection as a springboard to create your own history of training and advice for others.

Heidi Leatherby

HOW TO USE THIS BOOK

EVERY MAN'S HEART ONE DAY BEATS ITS FINAL BEAT. HIS LUNGS BREATHE THEIR FINAL BREATH. AND IF WHAT THAT MAN DID IN HIS LIFE MAKES THE BLOOD PULSE THROUGH THE BODY OF OTHERS AND MAKES THEM BELIEVE DEEPER IN SOMETHING THAT'S LARGER THAN LIFE, THEN HIS ESSENCE, HIS SPIRIT, WILL BE IMMORTALIZED BY THE STORYTELLERS - BY THE LOYALTY, BY THE MEMORY OF THOSE WHO HONOR HIM, AND MAKE THE RUNNING THE MAN DID LIVE FOREVER.
— JAMES BRIAN HELLWIG

Before you begin, I'd like to address some important points
for all to be aware of prior to working through this book.

1. Consult your physician before embarking on any physically demanding routine, this one included.

2. The internet is your friend. Because I did not want to reinvent the wheel by adding another 300+ pages to explain each movement in this book, I am directing you to your handy internet browser of choice to locate the movements if you have questions on how to perform them. This will also give you the chance to see a magnitude of ways to scale a movement to make it easier or more challenging. Please take your time to read through the workout of the day before delving into it, so that you are familiar with each movement ahead of time. I have included a basic Glossary of Terms

at the end of this book, in case you might be interested in learning about some of the movements described in the *Original Sessions*. Aside from that, I encourage you to research any prescribed movements you have questions about, as well as options for scaled or more challenging versions.

3. You are encouraged to adjust the number of repetitions as needed. Do not skip a training session because the workout looks too hard or too easy. Planned rest days are encouraged, but do not skip a day simply because you don't feel like it. If you can only do 10 repetitions of a prescribed set of 30, do 10. Shoot for 12 next time. If push-ups are rough for you, start on your knees. If squats and lunges hurt your knees, you're doing them wrong. Research proper form for all movements and get it right (your body will thank you). Again, there are a multitude of ways to adjust each and every movement; just consult the internet for ways to make them best fit your requirements, and push yourself a bit further each day to get better. On the flip side, if 100 burpees are a walk in the park for you, GOOD. Do 200. Add a weighted vest if 200 burpees are still too easy, or add 50 pound dumbbells and do 100 man makers instead. Scaling up doesn't have to be that drastic. Add dumbbells, weight plates, kettlebells, resistance bands, a pull-up bar, stones, water jugs, your cat, or any equipment you'd like. Be creative with these if the base movements are not challenging enough.

4. Be creative in using this book too. The training sessions do not progress in any linear way from easy to hard. They are varied on purpose, based on the original sessions performed. With that said, feel free to flip to any day randomly, and do that training session out of sheer luck. Use an online number randomizer from 1 - 365 and let that decide your fate for the day. Whatever way you choose to use this book, you cannot go wrong.

5. You'll find that some of the sessions are timed against a running clock, or will have rounds of exercises performed at the start of each minute for a certain number of minutes. I like using the free app called "WOD Timer" which allows for you to set up any amount of minutes, rounds, and length of rounds with ease. If anything, you'll need to utilize a stopwatch or the built in clock/stopwatch on your phone to make sure you're working for the prescribed amount of time rather than just guessing.

6. For the complainers who say the workouts are repetitive, GOOD. That's the point. You will see that all of the *Original Sessions* completed with my comrades over the months and years are not in any way new, exciting, or fun. Those workouts all consisted of the same work, over and over, for months and years on end. And this is what you are going to do, just like all of the great athletes before us have done day after day, year after year. What you have here, is just one year's worth, which is only the beginning. All of this is work at a core level and is meant to be done consistently. Don't let yourself use the 'I'm bored' excuse as you move through this book. You are not a child with a 15 minute attention span, and I am confident that, as an adult with full control over your mind, you can find ways to push through and do the work regardless of whether or not you find it boring. Just work. Come back tomorrow, and work some more. Reflect upon the quotes provided in this book as you work and as you go about your day.

7. Honor and be grateful for your accomplishments. Wash, rinse, and repeat.

8. Do NOT ask how long it takes to see and feel results. If you're asking that already, you're sinking yourself. Instead of asking yourself, "How long will it take?" ask yourself this:

How Far Can I Go?

WARMING UP, STRETCHING, AND COOL DOWNS

I did not include formal warm-ups, stretches, and cool downs within these individual training sessions because this varies depending on the individual. I highly recommend that you go through a small routine of your choice depending on your needs, but this should be different for everyone. Here is an example of what I might do as a warm up and cool down, but I encourage you to search the internet for various ways that might best target your specific areas of concern and apply daily.

- Warm-up: 30 - 60 seconds each of: light jog in place, jumping jacks, slow push-ups, shoulder rolls, neck rolls, knee circles, instep stretch, quad stretch, ankle circles, wrist circles
- Cool down: pick any area that may be tight or giving you trouble, and do a search for effective stretches and mobility that can be done for each.
- The book *Becoming a Supple Leopard* by Kelly Starrett is THE comprehensive manual of mobility and has been used by gyms and athletes for years as a go to manual for anything mobility related. At over 400 pages long, there is no area of the body that is ignored. I highly recommend this book, or any content by the author if you have questions regarding pain points as you move through your fitness journey.

THE TRAINING SESSIONS

DAY 1

IF IT'S IMPORTANT, DO IT EVERY DAY. — DAN GABLE

Original Session: Warm up: 2 rounds: 1 minute assault bike, 5 box jumps, 5 hang cleans, 20 kettlebell swings. Work to a heavy squat clean. Then, at the top of each minute for 10 minutes, perform 2 barbell cleans at a heavy but sustainable weight. At minute 12, take a 200 meter jog. Upon return, perform 2 rounds of: 20 kettlebell swings, 10 burpees. Finish off with 2 rounds of: 10 toes to bar, and 10 GHD hip extensions.

Home Edition:

- 30 air squats
- 2 minute jog (may substitute jogging in place)
- 20 burpees
- 2 minute jog (may substitute jogging in place)
- 10 sit ups

Perform 1-3 rounds of the above sequence and enjoy!

DAY 2

Original Session: Warm up: 2 rounds: 200 meter run, 5 pull-ups, 10 push-ups, 15 air squats. Work to a heavy deadlift. Perform repetitions of 10, 9, 8, 7, 6, 5, 4, 3, 2, 1 in the bodyweight deadlift, and pull-ups (10 deadlifts, 10 pull-ups, 9 deadlifts, 9 pull-ups until finished). Rest. Finish with 5 sets of 250 meter sprints on the rower.

Home Edition:

- Perform repetitions of 10, 9, 8, 7, 6, 5, 4, 3, 2, 1 of jump squats and push-ups (10 jump squats, 10 push-ups, 9 jump squats, 9 push-ups until finished)
- Take a few sprints around your block totalling 10 minutes (may substitute with 30 second intervals of jumping jacks - do this 5-10 times)
- Core work: Complete movement 1 for 10 repetitions, movement 2 for 10 repetitions, movement 1 for 9 repetitions, movement 2 for 9 repetitions. Continue until 1 repetition of each is complete
- Movement 1: V-ups (may substitute sit-ups)
- Movement 2: Spiderman planks

DAY 3

Original Session: Warm up of choice, then, Deck of 52 playing cards, plus 2 jokers. Suit determines the exercise, card value determines the number of repetitions (face cards = 10, Aces = 11).

- Hearts = Kettlebell swings
- Diamonds = Sit-Ups
- Clubs = Air Squats
- Spades = Box jumps (24/20 in)
- Jokers = 15 Burpees

Home Edition:

Grab a few friends and go through the whole deck, or if short on time, split the deck into segments and work through in smaller portions (face cards = 10 repetitions, Aces = 11 repetitions).

- Hearts = push-ups
- Diamonds = Sit-Ups
- Clubs = Air Squats
- Spades = Mountain Climbers
- Jokers = 15 Burpees

DAY 4

Original Session: Warm up - 2 minute row, then 2 rounds: 10 air squats, 5 push-ups, 5 push presses. 3 barbell military press, 3 push press (repeat for 7 rounds, up in weight each round). Then, 30 seconds kettlebell goblet squats, 30 seconds kettlebell swings, 30 seconds assault bike, 30 seconds rest (repeat for 8 rounds). Finish with 12 weighted sit-ups, 1 minute heavy farmer carries, 10 superman holds (repeat for 3 rounds).

Home Edition:

- Accumulate 3 rounds of 30 second handstand push-ups or handstand holds against a wall (may omit depending on skill level)
- 30 seconds each: push-ups, air squats, jumping jacks, plank, 1-2 minute rest (repeat for 8 rounds)
- 30 sit ups
- 30 second superman, 30 second glute bridge right, 30 second glute bridge left (repeat for 3 rounds)

DAY 5

Original Session: Warm up - 2 rounds: 30 second jump rope, 5 deadlifts, 5 power cleans, 5 front squats. Work to a heavy power clean. Then, 5 rounds of 1 power clean, one hang power clean. Finish with repetitions of 30-20-10 box jumps, push-ups, calorie row.

Home Edition:

- 20 burpees (repeat 2-3 times if desired)
- Take a jog around the block (may substitute 2 minute jog in place or jump rope)
- Complete repetitions of 30-20-10 of jump squats, push-ups, sit ups (30 jump squats, 30 push-ups, 30 sit-ups, 20 jump squats, 20 push-ups, 20 sit-ups, 10 jump squats, 10 push-ups, 10 sit ups)

DAY 6

Original Session: Warm up - 3 rounds; 30 second jump rope, sumo stretch, dislocates, 10 overhead squats. Work to a heavy overhead squat. Then complete 5 rounds of 1 overhead squat at 90% of maximum effort. Next, at the top of every minute for 10 minutes, perform 5 pull-ups, 10 push-ups, and 15 air squats. Finish with 150 slam balls with a partner.

Home Edition:

- 50 air squats (modify by placing hands behind head or arms overhead for a more difficult version)
- 5 sit-up v-ups, 10 mountain climbers, 15 second plank (repeat for 5 rounds)
- 30 seconds high knees, 30 seconds butt kickers (repeat for 3 rounds)

DAY 7

Original Session: Warm up - 250 meter row. 2 rounds: 5 front squats, 5 squat cleans, 5 box jumps, sumo stretch, sink stretch. Work to a heavy hang squat clean. 4 rounds at 50% of maximum effort: 6 hang squat clean, 200 meter run, 2 minute rest. Then, at the top of every minute, 4 burpees, using remaining time to complete as many kettlebell swings as possible. Athlete is done when they have accumulated 150 kettlebell swings, stopping at the top of every minute to do 4 burpees.

Home Edition:

- 10 minute jog (may substitute with running in place, jumping jacks, jump rope, or any combination of the above for 10 minutes)
- At the top of every minute, complete 4 burpees. With remaining time, complete as many lunges as possible. Athlete is done when 100 lunges are complete, stopping at the top of each minute to complete 4 burpees.

DAY 8

> *WHEN YOU HAVE WORKED HARD ALL DAY THIS IS YOUR OWN TIME WHEN YOU SHOULD BE HAVING FUN AND GETTING FIT. EXERCISE SHOULDN'T FEEL LIKE A CHORE. IT SHOULD BE FUN. THIS IS YOUR RELEASE.* — SAMANTHA BRIGGS

Original Session: Warm up - 2 rounds: 200 meter run, 5 pull-ups, 10 push-ups, 15 air squats, pigeon stretch, dislocates. With barbell: 3 push press, 9 ring rows (6 rounds, up in weight each round). Then complete 6 rounds of: 5 deadlifts, 10 air squats, 30 second assault bike sprint, 30 seconds rest. Finish with a 500 meter row under the assigned time.

Home Edition:

- Accumulate a total of 5 minutes handstand hold (may substitute plank, side plank, or other plank variation)
- 5 push-ups, 10 jump squats, 30 jumping jacks (repeat for 6 rounds)
- Finish with a 5 minute jog around your neighborhood (may substitute for jogging in place or jump rope)

DAY 9

> *CYNICS DON'T WANT RESULTS; THEY WANT AN EXCUSE TO NOT TAKE ACTION. IRONICALLY, EVEN IF THEY WIN THEIR OWN MANUFACTURED ARGUMENT, THEY LOSE OVERALL, BECAUSE THEY'RE STUCK IN A PRISON OF THEIR MIND. — RAMIT SETHI*

Original Session: Warm up - 100 meter row, sumo stretch. 3 rounds: 10 air squats, 10 push-ups, dislocates. Work to a heavy push press. Next, complete 5 rounds of 5 push presses at 60% of maximum effort, 5 ring rows. Then, complete 6 rounds of 15 goblet squats, 200 meter run. Finish with 3 rounds of 10 Romanian deadlifts, pigeon stretch, foam roll.

Home Edition:

- 5 rounds of 5 burpees
- 6 rounds of 15 air squats, jog around the block (or 2 minute jog in place)
- 3 rounds of 10 mountain climbers, 10 sit-ups
- Core work: Complete movement 1 for 10 repetitions, movement 2 for 10 repetitions, movement 1 for 9 repetitions, movement 2 for 9 repetitions. Continue until 1 repetition of each is complete
- Movement 1: Standing oblique crunch
- Movement 2: Spiderman planks

DAY 10

Original Session: Warm up - 2 rounds: 1 minute assault bike, 10 box jumps, 10 kettlebell swings, 10 air squats, elevated pigeon stretch, trap stretch. Complete 4 rounds of 25 kettlebell swings, 200 meter sprint, 1 minute rest. Follow with 4 rounds of 20 push-ups, 30 second assault bike sprint, 1 minute rest. Finish with athlete's choice of: 40 burpees, 75 ball slams, or 100 air squats.

Home Edition:

- 2-4 rounds of 20 lunges, jog around your block (may substitute for 2 minute jog in place)
- 2-4 rounds of 20 push-ups, 40 jumping jacks
- Finish with athlete's choice of: 40 burpees, 80 sit ups, or 100 air squats

DAY 11

Original Session: Warm up - 2 rounds: 60 second assault bike, 10 front squats, 10 push presses, couch stretch. Work to a heavy front squat. Rest. Complete 3 rounds of 1 front squat at 90% of maximum effort. Then, 7 rounds of 5 deadlifts, 5 hang squat cleans, and 5 thrusters. Finish with 3 rounds of 60 second grip plate carries.

Home Edition:

- 100 air squats, rest as needed
- 4 rounds of 5 push-ups, 10 flutter kicks, 15 sit ups
- Finish with max plank hold

DAY 12

Original Session: Warm up - 2 rounds: 5 pull-ups, 10 kettlebell swings, 15 air squats, sump stretch, dislocates. Work to heavy deadlift. Complete 6 rounds of 3 deadlifts at 70-80% of maximum effort. Then, athletes transition into 6 rounds of 250 meter sprint on the rower, with 1 minute rest between rounds. Finish with accumulating 5 minutes in handstand hold.

Home Edition:

- 2 rounds, 30 seconds each: alternating between high knees and moving push-ups (can substitute for push-ups)
- 2 rounds of 20 sit ups
- 1-3 rounds - take a jog around the block, or complete 2 minutes of jogging in place
- Accumulate 5 minutes in handstand hold

DAY 13

MY BIGGEST TAKEAWAY WAS THAT DOING MY ABSOLUTE BEST IS THE IDEAL OUTCOME. I REALIZED I DIDN'T HAVE TO DO ANYTHING SPECIAL. I JUST HAD TO WORK AS HARD AS I COULD WORK. I REALIZED I'M ONLY IN COMPETITION WITH MYSELF. IT WAS AROUND THIS TIME THAT I BEGAN TO INTERNALIZE THE SLOGAN, "BE THE BEST ME." — KATRIN DAVIDSDOTTIR

Original Session: Warm up - 2 rounds: 250 meter row, 10 military press, 10 air squats, pigeon stretch, instep stretch. With a kettlebell: 5 military press, 8 bent over row each arm. Then, execute 6 rounds of the following: 12 sandbag step-ups, 30 second assault bike sprint, 30 second rest. Next, complete 10 weighted sit-ups, and 10 barbell good mornings. 2 minute couch stretch each leg.

Home Edition:

- 4 rounds of 30 seconds side plank each arm
- 4 rounds of 30 seconds mountain climbers
- 50 lunges
- 40 sit ups (can vary with v-ups, bicycle crunches, and leg raises)
- 30 air squats

DAY 14

Original Session: Warm up - 2 rounds: 200 meter row, 10 push presses, 10 air squat, elevated pigeon stretch, sink stretch. Complete 6 rounds of 3 deadlifts, 1 heavy sled pull (increase weight each movement each round). Then, 6 rounds of 1 minute rower sprint, 2 minute rest. Finish with 4 minutes accumulated in a plank position of choice.

Home Edition:

- 4 rounds of 1 minute mountain climbers, 1 minute jumping jacks (or jump rope)
- Take a 10 minute run or accumulate 6-10 minutes jogging in place (may substitute for 50 burpees)
- Accumulate 4 minutes in plank position (rest as needed)

DAY 15

Original Session: Warm up - 2 rounds: 1 minute assault bike, 10 deadlifts, 10 push-ups, pigeon stretch. Work to a heavy deadlift. Then complete 5 rounds of 5 deadlifts, 100 meter sprint, walk back is the rest. Finish with 10-20-30 of box jumps, kettlebell swings, wall balls.

Home Edition:

- Complete the following circuit 3 times
- 50 squat jumps
- 40 sit ups
- 30 high knees
- 20 plank punches (10 each side)
- 10 side plank dips

DAY 16

Original Session: Warm up - 500 meter row. Complete 6 rounds of 3 power cleans, up in weight each round. Then finish with 6 rounds of maximum handstand holds, maximum push-ups, maximum ring rows, and maximum one leg broad jumps.

Home Edition:

- 30 speed skaters, 10 hand release burpees
- 30 jumping lunges, 50 mountain climbers
- 20 star jumps, 20 heisman
- Core work: Complete movement 1 for 10 repetitions, movement 2 for 10 repetitions, movement 1 for 9 repetitions, movement 2 for 9 repetitions. Continue until 1 repetition of each is complete. Movement 1: Walking toe touch, Movement 2: Spiderman plank

DAY 17

Original Session: Warm up - 2 rounds: 5 pull-ups, 10 box jumps, 15 air squats, 200 meter row. Work to a heavy deadlift. Then, perform 4 rounds of: 5 deadlift, 60 second row or assault bike sprint. Finish with as many rounds as possible in 12 minutes of: 400 meter run, 20 kettlebell swings, 20 box jumps, 20 air squats.

Home Edition:

- 100 pulsing squats
- 5 minute jog outside or jog in place indoors
- 50 burpees
- 3 rounds of 8 glute bridge pulses each side
- 3 rounds of 30 second side plank holds each side

DAY 18

Original Session: Warm up - 3 minutes each: foam roll, dislocates, sumo stretch. For 5 minutes: 20 seconds push-ups, 20 seconds rest, 20 seconds air squats, 20 seconds rest. Then, 20 minutes of power clean technique work, up in weight to heavy. Finish with 10,9,8,7,6,5,4,3,2,1 repetitions of kettlebell swing, (x2) sit-ups, and jump lunges.

Home Edition:

- Complete 5 rounds, 2 minutes each:
- 10 burpees
- Run around block or 2 minute jog in place
- Maximum repetition burpees

DAY 19

Original Session: Warm up - 5 minutes: 30 seconds jump rope, 30 seconds stretch. Work up to a heavy hang squat clean, then for 10 minutes, at the top of each minute, perform 2 hang cleans. Next, complete 6 rounds of: 60 seconds row or assault bike, 60 seconds rest, 200 meter run.

Home Edition:

- 15 minute jog (may substitute for 100 burpees)
- Mountain climbers
- 50-40-30-20-10 repetitions of the following:
- Mountain climbers
- Sit-ups

DAY 20

Original Session: Warm up - 5 minutes: 20 seconds air squats, 20 seconds push-ups, 20 seconds rest. 5 rounds of 5 military press (up in weight) and 10 plank rows. As many rounds as possible in 8 minutes of: 8 thrusters and 8 burpees. 3 rounds of 12 toes to bar, 60 sec rest between rounds.

Home Edition:

- 5 rounds of 3 wall walk-outs, 30 second side planks each side
- Accumulate 5 minutes of jumping jacks or jump rope
- 5 rounds of 5 leg raises, 10 flutter kicks, 20 sit-ups

DAY 21

IF YOU THINK YOU ARE ONLY STRONG IF YOU CAN LIFT A CERTAIN NUMBER, WHATEVER THAT NUMBER IS, YOU WILL FEEL PRETTY WEAK MOST OF THE TIME. STRENGTH IS NOT A DATA POINT; IT'S NOT A NUMBER. IT'S AN ATTITUDE. — PAVEL TSATSOULINE

Original Session: Warm up - 5 deadlifts, 5 box jumps, 5 push ups, sumo stretch, lat stretch. Athletes will work to a heavy deadlift. For time, complete 5 rounds of: 4 deadlifts, 6 wall balls, and 200 meter run. Increase repetitions by 2 each round. Finish with 3 rounds of 1 minute each: front plank, side plank (30 seconds each side).

Home Edition:

- 5 rounds of: 4 jump squats, 6 lunges, jog around the block (may substitute 3 minutes jogging in place)
- 20 moving push-ups
- 3 rounds of: front plank, side plank (30 seconds each side)
- 3 rounds of: 30 seconds superman holds, 30 seconds hollow holds

DAY 22

> *IT'S THAT GREAT FEELING, LIKE THE FIRST MAN ON THE MOON, THE FIRST MAN TO RUN A MILE IN UNDER FOUR MINUTES. AND NOW, I'M THE FIRST TO DEADLIFT HALF A TON. IT'S HISTORY, AND I'M VERY PROUD TO BE A PART OF IT. — EDDIE HALL*

Original Session: Warm up - At the top of each minute for 5 minutes: 5 push-ups, 5 air squats, 5 box jumps. Work to a heavy front squat. Then complete 5 rounds of: 3 front squats, 100 meter sprint, walk back is your rest. To finish, do 50-40-30-20-10 of the following movements: air squats, kettlebell swings, push-ups, and burpees.

Home Edition:

- 100 air squats
- 100 push-ups
- 100 sit-ups
- Athlete can divide the above into as many different segments, as long as all 300 repetitions are completed

DAY 23

Original Session: Warm up - 3 minute assault bike, then 2 rounds of: 5 deadlifts, 10 lunges each side, 10 push-ups, pigeon stretch. 5 rounds of the following movements: 5 deadlifts (up in weight each round) and 3 box jumps (up in height each round). Then, 6 rounds of the following: 8 sandbag jump squats, 50 step ups. Finish with 3 rounds of: banded side steps, (10 each side) 60 second plank, elevated glute bridge, (10 each side) 10 weighted sit-ups.

Home Edition:

- 6 rounds of: 10 jump squats, 50 lunges (25 each side)
- 10 inchworm to push-up
- 10 glute bridge walk outs
- 20 leg raises (may substitute for 50 sit ups)

DAY 24

Original Session: Warm up - 2 minute assault bike, then 2 rounds of: 10 air squats, 10 push-ups, 5 box jumps, dislocates, foam roll. For 10 minutes, 30 kettlebell swings, 30 seconds rest. Then perform 21-15-9 of the following: back squat, ring rows. Finally, complete 3 rounds of: 400 meter run, 150 jump rope repetitions.

Home Edition:

- For 20 minutes, 1 minute work, 1 minute rest: burpees
- 21-15-9 repetitions of: side dip planks, floor tricep dips
- 5 minute jog (may substitute 3 minutes jump rope or jumping jacks)

DAY 25

Original Session: Warm up - 1 minute assault bike, 10 lunges, 10 air squats, 10 push-ups. Work to a heavy deadlift. Then complete 3 rounds of: 10 deadlifts, 20 box jumps. Next, complete 100 sit ups. Finish with 3 rounds of: 10 overhead lunges, 10 Russian twists, 60 seconds farmers carry.

Home Edition:

- 30 shoulderstand squats
- 50 sit-ups
- 100 lunges (50 each side)
- 50 sit-ups

DAY 26

Original Session: Warm up - 40 wall balls, shoulder mobility. 3 rounds of: 10 bench press, 30 second row sprint, 30 second rest. 3 rounds of: 10 weighted lunges each side, 15 meter heavy sled drag. 3 rounds of: 8 pull-ups, 8 tricep dips, 8 push-ups, 8 sit-ups, 8 kettlebell swings.

Home Edition:

- 3 rounds of: 10 diamond push-ups, 30 second jumping jacks
- 3 rounds of: 10 air squats, 10 double leg raises
- 3 rounds of: 8 tricep dips, 8 sit-ups, 8 glute bridge walk outs

DAY 27

Original Session: Warm up - 3 minute assault bike, 3 rounds of: 10 kettlebell swings, 10 goblet squats, 3 jump squats, pigeon stretch, instep stretch. Work to a heavy power clean. Then, for 5 rounds complete 2 power cleans at 80% maximum effort. Next, complete front squats and burpees in the following repetition scheme: 10,9,8,7,6,5,4,3,2,1. Finish with 2 rounds of: 1 minute plank, couch stretch, sumo stretch.

Home Edition:

- Complete 10,9,8,7,6,5,4,3,2,1 of: jump squats and burpees (10 jump squats, 10 burpees, 9 jump squats, 9 burpees . . . until finished)
- 40 heismans, 40 jumping jacks, 40 butt kickers
- Accumulate 5 minutes in plank position (can be variation of front plank and side planks)

DAY 28

Original Session: Warm up - 3 minute assault bike, then at the top of every minute for 5 minutes: 5 push-ups, 5 air squats, 5 box jumps. Work to a heavy back squat. Then perform 6 rounds of 2 back squats at 80% maximum effort. Next, complete 5 rounds of 10 thrusters and 10 pull-ups. End with 3 rounds of 10 Romanian deadlifts.

Home Edition:

- 6 rounds of: 2 jump squats, jog around the block or 2 minutes jumping jacks
- 5 rounds of: 1 maximum handstand hold, 10 push-ups
- 3 rounds of: 1 minute sit ups, 1 minute plank, 1 minute standing oblique crunch (30 seconds each side)

DAY 29

Original Session: Warm up - 200 meter run, 5 deadlifts, 5 box jumps, 5 pull-ups. Work through 6 rounds of 3 deadlifts, up in weight each round. Then, against a 14 minute clock, perform even/odd of: 6 burpee box jumps, 12 wall ball shots. Finish with a partner 1500 meter row, 400 meter weighted sandbag run, 150 calorie assault bike.

Home Edition:

- 20 frog jumps (5 forward, 5 back, 5 forward, 5 back)
- Jog around the block (may substitute for 10 burpees, 10 high knees, 10 butt kickers)
- 20 frog jumps (5 forward, 5 back, 5 forward, 5 back)
- Jog around the block (may substitute for 10 burpees, 10 high knees, 10 butt kickers)
- Jog around the block (may substitute for 2:00 minute jog in place or 2:00 jumping jacks)
- 3 rounds: 10 moving push-ups, 20 sit-ups, 30 jumping lunges

DAY 30

Original Session: Warm up - 1 minute assault bike, 10 goblet squats, couch stretch. Increase weight to a heavy back squat. Then, complete 5 rounds of 5 back squat, one 15 meter heavy sled drag. 30-20-10 repetitions of: box jumps, kettlebell swing, wall ball shots. Finally, complete one 800 meter run.

Home Edition:

- 5 rounds of: 1 minute air squats, 1 minute burpees, 1 minute heismans
- 40-30-20-10 of: Mountain climbers, Sit-ups, push-ups, glute raises
- 3 rounds of: 1 minute wall sit holds

DAY 31

Original Session: Warm up - 5 minutes: 30 seconds on, 30 seconds off assault bike, stretch. Work to a heavy squat clean. Against a 5 minute clock, every 30 seconds complete: 1 squat clean at 70-80 percent maximum effort. Complete with a partner the following: 10,9,8,7,6,5,4,3,2,1 burpee box jumps, with a 150 meter row in between sets.

Home Edition:

- 100 jumping lunges (50 each side, rest as needed)
- 10,9,8,7,6,5,4,3,2,1 repetitions of: v-up sit ups, with a 2:00 block of jumping jacks, jogging in place, or jump rope in between each set.

DAY 32

Original Session: Warm up - 6 minutes: 30 seconds on/30 seconds off assault bike, stretch. pull-ups / push-up pyramid. Complete the following: 2 /5 , 4/10, 6/15, 8/20, 6/15, 4/10, 2 /5. Then, with the following repetition scheme, complete: box jumps, wall ball shots, kettlebell swings - 10,9,8,7,6,5,4,3,2,1. Finish with 3 rounds of: 1 minute side plank, (30 seconds each side) 20 Russian twists, 10 GHD hip extensions.

Home Edition:

- Push-up and sit-up pyramid: 2 push-ups /5 sit-ups , 4 push-ups/10 sit-ups, 6 push-ups/15 sit-ups, 8 push-ups/20 sit-ups, 6 sit-ups/15 push-ups, 4 sit-ups,/10 push-ups, 2 sit-ups /5 push-ups
- 40 single leg glute bridges (divide up as desired)
- 20 unweighted Russian twists

DAY 33

Original Session: Warm up - 3 rounds: 30 second air squat, 5 deadlifts, 5 squat cleans, 5 front squats, pigeon stretch. Work a heavy squat clean to front squat. Then, every minute on the minute for 8 minutes, complete 2 complexes of: 1 squat clean, 1 front squat. With a partner, 10 minutes of: 60 second assault bike sprint, 20 kettlebell swings. Finish with a 1 minute farmer's carry for 3 rounds.

Home Edition:

- 40 tuck jumps
- 10 minute run (may substitute for 100 burpees)
- 40 toe touches
- 10 minute run (may substitute for 100 sit ups)

DAY 34

Original Session: Warm up - 5 hang squat clean, 5 box jumps, 10 walking lunges, sumo stretch, dislocates. Work to a heavy squat clean, then complete 5 rounds of 1 squat clean at 90 percent of maximum effort. 4 rounds, 5 minutes each, as many repetitions as possible of: 3 box jumps, 6 dumbbell thrusters, 9 kettlebell swings. Complete elevated pigeon stretch and foam roll.

Home Edition:

- 5 rounds of: 10 single leg deadlift reach, 10 side lunges, 10 glute bridges, 10 Bulgarian split squats
- Accumulate 5 minutes of handstand holds (may substitute 5 rounds of 3 walk walks)
- Jog around the block (may substitute 30 burpees)

DAY 35

Original Session: Warm up - 2 rounds: 1 minute assault bike, sumo stretch, instep stretch, 8 front squats. Then, complete 6 rounds, up in weight and height each round: 3 front squats, 3 box jumps. Next, as many rounds as possible in 10 minutes: 200 meter run, 25 double unders (75 single jump ropes) 10 thrusters. Finish with 30 seconds each of: right plank, left plank, front plank.

Home Edition:

- 3 rounds, one minute each movement: jump squats, diamond push-ups, ski abs
- 3 rounds, one minute each movement: reverse lunges, mountain climbers, standing oblique crunch (30 seconds each side)
- 3 rounds, one minute each movement: jump rope or jumping jacks, frog hops, v-ups or sit ups

DAY 36

Original Session: Warm up - 3 minutes each: Foam roll, stretch of choice. Then At the top of each minute for 5 minutes, 5 burpees, 4 gym length sprints. Work to a heavy thruster, followed by 8 minutes, at the top of each minute, perform 3 thrusters, 3 box jumps. Next, complete 4 rounds with a partner of: 60 second assault bike sprint, 60 second double front rack kettlebell hold (one partner bikes while other partner holds). 2 rounds: 20 GHD hip extensions.

Home Edition:

- At the top of each minute for 5 minutes: 5 burpees, 10 high knees
- 20 jump squats
- Jog around the block (may substitute 2 minutes jumping jacks or jump rope)
- 3 rounds: 10 single leg glute bridges, (5 each side) 10 tricep dips, 20 bicycle crunches

DAY 37

Original Session: Warm up - 4 minutes assault bike, 3 rounds: 10 back squat up in weight. 5 rounds: 5 back squat, then 10-9-8-7-6-5-4-3-2-1 repetitions of kettlebell movements: deadlift, row, clean, front squat, push press. Finish with 2 rounds of 15 GHD sit ups and 15 GHD hip extensions.

Home Edition:

- 10-9-8-7-6-5-4-3-2-1 repetitions of: push-ups, sit-ups, floor switch kicks (10 push-ups, 10 sit-ups, 10 floor switch kicks / 9push-ups, 9sit-ups, 9 floor switch kicks . . . until finished)
- Jog around block or 5 minute jog in place
- 30 side lunges (15 each side)
- 20 burpees

DAY 38

BEFORE SUCCESS COMES IN ANY MAN'S LIFE, HE IS SURE TO MEET WITH MUCH TEMPORARY DEFEAT, AND, PERHAPS, SOME FAILURE. WHEN DEFEAT OVERTAKES A MAN, THE EASIEST AND MOST LOGICAL THING TO DO IS TO QUIT. THAT IS EXACTLY WHAT THE MAJORITY OF MEN DO. MORE THAN FIVE HUNDRED OF THE MOST SUCCESSFUL MEN THIS COUNTRY HAS EVER KNOWN TOLD THE AUTHOR THEIR GREATEST SUCCESS CAME JUST ONE STEP BEYOND THE POINT AT WHICH DEFEAT HAD OVERTAKEN THEM — NAPOLEON HILL

Original Session: Warm up - 2 rounds: 1 minute assault bike, 5 deadlifts, 5 box jumps, 5 pull ups, sumo stretch, dislocates, foam roll. Work to heavy deadlift. Then, at the top of each minute for 8 minutes: 4 deadlifts, 4 burpees. Finish with 40,30,20,10 wall ball shots, double unders. If doing singles, triple the number of repetitions. 3 rounds Romanian deadlifts.

Home Edition:

- Complete 300 burpees today. Can be split up into as many segments throughout the day as desired.

DAY 39

Original Session: Warm up - 3 rounds: 5 box jumps, 5 hang squat clean, 5 push-ups, sumo stretch, lat stretch, instep stretch. Work to a heavy thruster, then complete 3 rounds of: 1 minute each station / 1 minute rest between rounds: push press, row, air squat, box jumps, ball slams or sledgehammer tire.

Home Edition:

- 50-40-30-20-10 repetitions of: stance jacks, butt kickers, high knees, frog jumps
- Abdominal circuit: 1 minute each: flutter kicks, sit ups, side plank with pulses, (30 seconds each side) double leg raises, superman hold, hollow hold, Russian twist, v-ups

DAY 40

YOU WILL ALWAYS MISS 100 PERCENT OF THE SHOTS YOU DON'T TAKE. — WAYNE GRETZKY

Original Session: Warm up - 3 minute assault bike, 2 rounds of: barbell complex - 5 deadlift, 5 row, 5 power clean, 5 front squat, 5 push press, 5 back squat, pigeon stretch, instep stretch. Work to a heavy power clean to thruster. Then, as many rounds as possible in: 5 minutes = 500 meter row, burpees to finish, 4 minutes = 500 meter row, pull-ups to finish, 3 minutes = 500 meter row, kettlebell swings rest of time.

Home Edition:

- 21-15-9 repetitions of: jump squats, push-ups
- 5 minute run (may substitute for 5 minutes jump rope or jogging in place)
- 21-15-9 repetitions of: tricep dips, super planks

DAY 41

I THINK THAT THE GOOD AND THE GREAT ARE ONLY SEPARATED BY THE WILLINGNESS TO SACRIFICE. — KAREEM ABDUL-JABBAR

Original Session: Warm up - 2 rounds: 1 minute row, 5 deadlifts, 10 walking lunges, 10 air squats, 10 push-ups, instep, pigeon stretch. Then complete 5 rounds of: 5 Romanian deadlifts, up in weight. Finish with a partner: 50 burpee pull-ups, 60 box jumps, 70 goblet squats, 80 dumbbell push press, 100 calorie assault bike. Resting partner holds a plank or performs overhead plate carries.

Home Edition:

- Buy In 30 Burpees
- 30 push-ups
- 40 walking lunges
- 50 mountain climbers
- 60 sit ups
- Buy out 30 Burpees

DAY 42

Original Session: Warm up - 2 rounds: 1 minute row, 10 air squats, 10 push-ups, 5 pull-ups, 5 box jumps. Then 1) 30 seconds row, 2) Chest to bar pull-ups, 3) Box jumps, 4) Burpees, 5) Toes to Bar, 6) Wall ball shots, 7) Kettlebell swings, 8) Weighted sit ups, 9) Ring rows, 10), Back squat. Add one movement to the bottom each time though to the top, repeat.

Home Edition:

- 1 minute jumping jacks
- 1 minute push-ups
- 1 minute jumping lunges
- 1 minute mountain climbers
- 1 minute sit ups
- 1 minute front plank
- 1 minute toe touches
- 1 minute side lunges
- Repeat the above for 7-8 rounds

DAY 43

Original Session: Warm up - 7 minutes, 30 seconds on / 30 seconds off assault bike. Work to a heavy back squat, then drop down to 70-80% maximum effort and complete 3 rounds of 3 back squats. Finally, complete 4 rounds of: as many repetitions as possible in 3 minute time blocks: 3 thrusters, 6 push-ups, 9 kettlebell swings

Home Edition:

- 5 rounds of 1 minute wall sit (or accumulate 5 minutes total with rest as needed)
- Complete as many possible rounds of the following in 3 minutes: 3 burpees, 6 push-ups, 9 sit-ups
- Complete as many possible rounds of the following in 3 minutes: 3 jump squats, 6 side to side push-ups, 9 v-ups
- Complete as many possible rounds of the following in 3 minutes: 3 frog jumps, 6 plank knee taps, 9 double leg raises

DAY 44

Original Session: Warm up - 2 rounds: 5 deadlifts, 5 push-ups, 5 box jumps, pigeon stretch, instep stretch. Complete 5 deadlifts, up in weight. Then, 5 rounds of: 10 burpees, 250 meter row. Finish with 3 rounds of: 1 minute plank, pigeon, roam roll, couch stretch.

Home Edition:

- 5 rounds of: 10 burpees, jog around the block (or 3 minutes jog in place)
- 3 rounds of 1 minute each: in and out abs, front plank, side plank, superman hold, hollow hold
- Finish with max handstand hold or wall handstand hold (try for a total of 3 minutes)

DAY 45

Original Session: Warm up - 1 minute jump rope, 5 thrusters, 5 push-ups, sumo stretch, dislocates. Then, work to a heavy one rep max thruster. 3 rounds of: 8 thrusters, (at 60% of maximum effort) 2 minute row. Then, every minute on the minute for 10 minutes: 8 kettlebell swings, 1 gym length sprint. Finish with a 60 second max assault bike sprint.

Home Edition:

- 5 rounds of: 8 non-weighted thrusters, 2 minute jog around the block or jog in place
- At the top of each minute for 10 minutes: 8 sit-ups, 1 burpee
- Finish with one 60 second max jumping jacks

DAY 46

Original Session: Warm up - 3 minute row, sumo stretch, instep stretch, pigeon. Next, the athlete works to a heavy front squat. Partner work: Movements are: Front squats, burpee box jumps. Must clean from the ground, no rack. Start with 3 of each, add 3 each round until 30 minutes is up.

Home Edition:

- Set a timer for 30 minutes and perform the following, adding 3 repetitions each time through until 30 minutes is up:
- Air squats, burpees.
- Repetitions will look similar to, 3 air squats, 3 burpees, 6 air squats, 6 burpees, 9 air squats, 9 burpees...until finished

DAY 47

Original Session: Warm up - 500 meter row, then 2 rounds of: 5 deadlifts, 10 walking lunges, 10 push-ups, sumo stretch, instep stretch. Work to a heavy deadlift, then perform 3 rounds of 2 deadlifts at 80% of maximum effort. Next, 4 rounds of: 9 deadlifts, 6 ring dips, 6 box jumps. Finish with 3 rounds of maximum romanian deadlifts, plank, superman holds.

Home Edition:

- 4 rounds of: 18 frog jumps, 12 tricep dips, 6 jumping lunges
- 40-30-20-10 repetitions of: sit-ups, spiderman planks, glute raises

DAY 48

Original Session: Warm up - 2 rounds of: 10 gym sprints, 5 back squats, 5 box jumps, sumo stretch, sink stretch. Work up to 50% of maximum back squat, then perform 6 rounds of: 3 back squats, working to 80% of maximum effort. Then at the top of every minute for 10 minutes - first minute - 20 kettlebell swings. Second minute - 10 burpees. Next, 21-15-9 repetitions of wall balls and box jumps.

Home Edition:

- 5 minute jog around your block or accumulate 5 minutes jumping jacks, high knees, and butt kickers
- At the top of every minute for 10 minutes - minute one - 20 air squats. Minute two - 10 burpees.
- 21-15-9 repetitions each of: in and out abs, side plank pulses (21-15-9 each side)

DAY 49

Original Session: Warm up - 5 overhead squats, 5 walking lunges, 5 pull-ups. Power snatch progression and technique work. Then, 6 rounds for time of: 5 pull-ups, 10 push press, 15 air squats. Finish with 3 rounds of 10 barbell good mornings.

Home Edition:

- 6 rounds of: 5 wall walks, 10 push-ups, 15 prisoner squats (hold arms straight overhead or hands behind head)
- 3 rounds of 30 stance jacks
- 2 rounds of 30 ground switch kicks (or tricep dips)
- 1 round of 30 flutter kicks

DAY 50

Original Session: Warm up - 5 rounds of: 5 push-ups, 5 air squats, 5 box jumps. Work to a heavy deadlift. Then, perform 4 rounds of: 3 deadlifts at 80% of maximum effort, gym length sprints. Row ladder: 1000 meters, 750 meters, 500 meters, 250 meters. 2 minute rest in between rounds.

Home Edition:

- 4 rounds of: 20 jump squats, 2 minute jog around your block or 2 minutes jumping jacks
- 100 burpees

DAY 51

ONE OF THE THINGS I LEARNED THE HARD WAY WAS THAT IT DOESN'T PAY TO GET DISCOURAGED. KEEPING BUSY AND MAKING OPTIMISM A WAY OF LIFE CAN RESTORE YOUR FAITH IN YOURSELF. — LUCILLE BALL

Original Session: Warm up - Kettlebell swing ladder - 10 each: 8k, 12k, 16k, 20k, 24k. Then, work up in weight to a heavy set of 4 back squats. Finish with 50 calorie assault bike, 40 dumbbell snatches, 30 toes to bar, 20 burpees, 10 pull-ups, 10 push-ups. Foam roll, t-spine smash.

Home Edition:

- Walking lungess ladder: 8, 12, 16, 20, 24, 20, 16, 12, 8
- 10 minute jog around your block, or accumulate 10 minutes of (straight arm jumping jacks, heismans, high knees, standing oblique crunches, sprinting in place)
- 40 windmills, 30 v-up sit ups, (or 30 leg raises) 20 burpees, 10 tricep dips, 10 push-ups

DAY 52

Original Session: Warm up - 4 minute row. Then, work to a heavy deadlift. Drop to 80% of maximum effort and perform 4 rounds of 3 deadlifts. With a partner, finish with 4 minutes of max wall balls, and 7 minutes of max row for distance.

Home Edition:

- Max toe tap mountain climbers in 4 minutes
- 5 rounds, 1 minute each: Jump rope, (or substitute with jumping jacks) shoulder tap planks, power jumps, scissor kicks

DAY 53

Original Session: Warm up - 5 front squats, 5 hang cleans, 5 box jumps, pigeon stretch, instep stretch. Work to a heavy squat clean. Then, at the top of every minute for 8 minutes, perform 2 squat cleans at 80% of maximum effort, 2 box jumps. Finish with 50, 40, 30, 20, 10 of: kettlebell swings, walking lunges, double unders (if doing singles, triple the amount).

Home Edition:

- Roll the dice: 1 = flutter kicks, 2 = jumping lunges, 3 = jump rope or hop in place, 4 = sit-ups, 5 = walking plank push-ups, 6 = wall sit
- Each movement is performed for 30 seconds, set clock for a total of 30 minutes of work.

DAY 54

Original Session: Warm up - 5 minutes: 30 seconds on, 30 seconds off jump rope, stretch of choice. Then, 6 rounds of 5 back squats, up in weight each round. Next, complete 3 rounds, 4 minutes each (as many repetitions as possible in 4 minutes): 5 thrusters, 10 pull-ups or push-ups, 15 kettlebell swings. Finish with 2 minutes of calf smashes each side, 2 minutes couch stretch each side

Home Edition:

- Buy in: 50 air squats
- 3 rounds, 4 minutes each. As many repetitions possible in each 4 minute round of: 5 unweighted thrusters, 10 push-ups, 15 flutter kicks
- Buy out: 50 air squats

DAY 55

Original Session: Warm up - 500 meter row, then 2 rounds of: 5 walking lunges, 10 air squats, 10 push presses, dislocates, instep stretch. Then, complete 20 walking overhead lunges with snatch grip kettlebells or plate, 30 second row sprint. Next, 3 rounds of: 10 deadlifts, up in weight, 30 seconds box jumps, 30 seconds rest. Finish with 30 weighted sit ups, 40 wall balls, 50 assault bike calories.

Home Edition:

- Jog around your block or run in place for 3 minutes.
- 50 jumping jacks
- 50 lunges (forward or backward, your choice)
- 50 sit-ups
- 50 glute bridges
- 50 reverse sit-ups
- 50 jumping jacks

DAY 56

Original Session: Warm up - 2 rounds: 1 minute row or assault bike, 5 box step ups, 10 deadlifts, pigeon stretch, sumo stretch. Work to a heavy deadlift, then complete 4 deadlifts at 90% of maximum effort. Next, with a partner complete: 10,9,8,7,6,5,4,3,2,1 of: double kettlebell deadlift, double kettlebell cleans, double kettlebell squat, double kettlebell press. Finish with 3 rounds of 10 GHD sit ups or weighted sit-ups.

Home Edition:

- 10 min Jumping jacks
- 10 rounds: 10 Jumping jacks, 10 push-ups
- 100 alternating lunges
- 110 sit-ups
- 2 rounds: 55 push-up to plank
- 55 sit-ups
- 3 rounds: 10 jumping jacks,10 push-ups

DAY 57

Original Session: Warm up - 2 rounds: 1 minute assault bike, 5 back squats, 5 walking lunges, pigeon stretch, 5 box jumps. Then, work to a heavy back squat. Drop to 80% of maximum effort and complete 3 rounds of 2 back squats. Finish with 40-30-20-10 wall balls and push-ups.

Home Edition:

- 5 minute jog around the block or 5 minutes jumping jacks
- 10-20-30-40-30-20-10 repetitions of: air squats, sit- ups, push-ups
- 1 minute each of: front plank, side plank raises, (30 seconds each side) flutter kicks, hollow hold, superman, flutter kicks, standing oblique crunch (30 seconds each side)

DAY 58

Original Session: Warm up - 7 minutes: 30 seconds on/30 seconds off assault bike. Then work to 60% of maximum effort deadlift. Next, complete 5 rounds of 5 deadlifts, up in weight each round. Then, 3 rounds, one minute each of: wall balls, push press, kettlebell swings, box jumps, row. One minute rest between full rounds.

Home Edition:

- Accumulate 3 minutes each of: handstand holds (may substitute wall walks) wall sits
- 3 rounds of one minute each: reverse lunges, push-ups, sit-ups, power jumps, high knees
- Finish with max plank hold (try for 3-5 minutes minimum)

DAY 59

THE FUTURE REWARDS THOSE WHO PRESS ON. I DON'T HAVE TIME TO FEEL SORRY FOR MYSELF. I DON'T HAVE TIME TO COMPLAIN. I'M GOING TO PRESS ON.
— BARACK OBAMA

Original Session: Warm up - 10 kettlebell swings, 10 box jumps, 10 walking lunges, 10 overhead squats. Then, complete 3 rounds of: 8 overhead squats, 50 calorie row or assault bike, one minute rest. Next, 3 rounds of: 8 hang power cleans, 1 minute gym sprints, 45 second rest. Finally, 3 rounds of battle rope complex: 20 alternating slams, 20 side to side, 20 double slams, 20 jumping jacks.

Home Edition:

- 3 rounds of: 8 arms overhead squats, (or hands behind head) 5 minute jog around your block or jog in place
- 3 rounds of: 20 power jumps, 40 jumping jacks
- 3 rounds of: 20 stance jacks, 20 ski abs, 20 frog jumps, 20 tricep dips

DAY 60

Original Session: 35 minute row for distance

Home Edition:

- 35 minute run OR
- 5 minutes each: jog in place, jumping jacks, high knees, butt kickers, heisman, standing oblique crunch, power jumps

DAY 61

Original Session: Warm up - 3 minute assault bike, then 2 rounds of: 5 front squats, 5 hang squat cleans, pigeon stretch, instep stretch. Work to a heavy complex: power clean, hang squat clean. Then complete 5 rounds of 1 complex at 80% of maximum effort. Next, with a partner complete: 21-18-15-12-9-6-3 repetitions of wall balls and kettlebell swings. FInish with couch stretch and calf smash.

Home Edition:

- Perform the following repetition scheme with these movements: unweighted thrusters, plank jacks, sit-ups, walking lunges
- 21-18-15-12-9-6-3-6-9-12-15-18-21

DAY 62

Original Session: Warm up - 500 meter row, 2 rounds of: 10 dislocates, 10 overhead squats, 10 push press, 10 overhead lunges, sumo stretch. Then, work to a heavy overhead squat. Following that, drop to 80% of maximum effort and complete 3 sets of 1 overhead squat. Then, from 0-5 minutes on the clock, perform 45 burpee box jumps. From 5-10 minutes complete 70 wall balls. Rest of time is 21-15-9 pull ups and backs squats.

Home Edition:

- For 5 minutes, perform as many burpee to power jumps as possible
- For 5 minutes, perform as many air squats as possible
- Finish with 21-15-9 of push-ups, sit-ups, and mountain climbers

DAY 63

IT'S NOT ALWAYS NECESSARY TO BE STRONG, BUT TO FEEL STRONG. — JON KRAKAUER

Original Session: Warm up - 2 rounds: 1 minute assault bike, 15 kettlebell swings, 10 air squats, elevated pigeon, sink stretch. Then, work to a heavy deadlift. Next, complete three rounds of: 10 deadlifts @65K, 100 jump rope, 2 minutes rest. Finish with: 30, 20, 10 box jumps, ring rows, clean and press.

Home Edition:

- Run 1 mile
- 100 air squats
- 100 push-ups
- Run 1 mile

DAY 64

WITH THE NEW DAY COMES NEW STRENGTH AND NEW THOUGHTS. — ELEANOR ROOSEVELT

Original Session: Warm up - 2 rounds of: 10 kettlebell swings, 10 box jumps, 10 gym length sprints, dislocates, instep. Work to a heavy front squat. Then, complete 5 rounds of 2 front squats. Finish with 21-15-9 wall balls, toes to bar, overhead lunges.

Home Edition:

- 3 rounds of 10 repetitions each: power jumps, stance jacks, side lunges
- 50 burpees
- 21-15-9 repetitions of: sit ups, leg raises, flutter kicks

DAY 65

Original Session: Warm up - 2 rounds of: 1 minute assault bike, 10 kettlebell swings, 5 box jumps, 10 push-ups, 10 walking lunges. 6 rounds - 5-6 strict pull-ups. 4 rounds - 250 meter row, 30 kettlebell swings, 20 wall balls, 10 box jumps. 3 rounds - battle rope complex: 20 each: slams, alternates, side to side, jumping jacks

Home Edition:

- 6 rounds of: 3 wall walks OR 30 second handstand holds
- 4 rounds of: jog around block, (or 3 minutes jog in place) 30 mountain climbers, 20 air squats, 10 frog jumps
- 3 rounds of: 50 jumping jacks, 1 minute plank

DAY 66

Original Session: Warm up - 2 rounds - 30 second jump rope, 10 air squats, 10 push-ups, 10 side lunges, instep stretch. Then, 5 rounds of 1 back squat (up in weight each round) 3 box jumps. Partner row - each person completes: 500 meter, 400 meter, 300 meter, 200 meter, 100 meter. Wall ball 2 for 1: 30-20-10. Finish with a 100 calorie assault bike or 2 minutes each.

Home Edition:

- Jog ladder: (either jog in place or use minutes spent outside) 5 minutes, 4 minutes, 3 minutes, 2 minutes, 1 minute. Perform 10 push-ups in between rounds.
- 30-20-10 Air squats. Perform 10 sit-ups in between each round.
- Finish with5 minute jog around your block or 5 minutes jumping jacks.

DAY 67

Original Session: Warm up - 3 minutes row, then kettlebell complex: 10 swings at each weight: 12, 18, 26, 35, 44, 52#. Work up in weight to a heavy set of 1 hang squat clean and 2 front squats. Then, complete 5 rounds of 1 hang squat clean and 2 front squats. Next, 90 second assault bike, 10 deadlifts, 20 box jumps, 30 sit-ups, 90 second assault bike, 10 deadlifts, 20 wall balls, 90 jump rope, 90 second assault bike, 10 deadlifts, 20 push-ups, 30 air squats, 90 seconds assault bike.

Home Edition:

- 5 rounds of 10 jump squats, 10 overhead lunges (5/5 each side)
- 90 seconds jump rope or jumping jacks, 10 ski abs, 20 burpees, 30 sit-ups, 90 seconds jump rope or jumping jacks, 10 ski abs, 20 air squats, 90 seconds jump rope or jumping jacks, 10 ski abs, 20 push-ups, 30 air squats, 90 seconds jump rope or jumping jacks

DAY 68

Original Session: Warm up - 2 rounds: 1 minute assault bike, 5 hang squat cleans, 5 box jumps, 10 lateral band steps. Then, complete 3 rounds of 8 hang squat cleans, 200 meter run, 1 minute rest. Next, 3 rounds of 8 back squats, 1 minute box jumps. Finish with 7 rounds of 10 kettlebell swings, 10 burpees.

Home Edition:

- 3 rounds of: 20 jumping lunges, jog around block or 3 minute jog in place
- 3 rounds of: 20 air squats, 1 minute stance jacks
- 5 rounds of: 20 burpees (rest as needed between rounds)

DAY 69

Original Session: Warm up - 200 meter run, 5 front squats, 10 jumping pull-ups, 15 kettlebell swings, band progression. Work to a heavy squat clean. Then at the top of each minute for 8 minutes: 2 squat cleans at 70-80% of maximum effort. Finish with ladder of: 500 meter row, 18 overhead squats, 400 meter row, 12 overhead squats, 300 meter row, 9 overhead squats

Home Edition:

- 40 burpees
- 5 minute run/jog in place, 50 squats with arms overhead, 4 minute run/jog in place, 40 push-ups, 3 minute run/jog in place, 30 v-up sit ups

DAY 70

Original Session: Warm up - 500 meter row, then 2 rounds of 5 push-ups, 10 lunges, 10 air squats, pigeon stretch, instep stretch. Work to a heavy thruster. Then, at 80% of maximum effort, perform 3 thrusters. Next, complete 21-15-9 thrusters and pull-ups. Finish with 3 rounds of banded air squats, L-sit holds, 10 superman pulses.

Home Edition:

- 5 minute jog around block or 5 minutes jump rope/jog in place
- 4 rounds: 5 push-ups, 10 lunges, 10 air squats
- 21-15-9 burpees and seconds spent in handstand hold
- 3 rounds: 1 minute wall sit, 30 second hollow hold, 30 second superman hold

DAY 71

Original Session: Warm up - 2 rounds: 1 minute assault bike, 10 lunges, 5 strict presses, 5 push presses. Work to a heavy strict press and push press combination of 3 repetitions each. Then complete 4 rounds of 3 strict presses. Next, complete as many rounds as possible in 6 minutes of: 3 pull-ups, 6 goblet squats, 9 box jumps. Finish with as many rounds as possible in 6 minutes of: 15 calorie row, 10 burpees.

Home Edition:

- 4 rounds: 10 push-ups, 10 air squats
- Against a 6 minute clock, as many rounds as possible of: 3 burpees, 6 jumping lunges, 9 stance jacks
- 6 rounds: 2 minute jog in place 10 glute bridge walk outs

DAY 72

Original Session: Warm up - 250 meter row, 5 back squat, 10 push-ups, 15 kettlebell swings. Then work to a heavy back squat. 20 super squats. 5 rounds: 7 deadlifts, 14 toes to bar, 21 weighted sit ups.

Home Edition:

- 5 minute jog around your block or accumulate 5 minutes jogging in place, jumping jacks, or jump rope.
- 150 air squats
- 100 sit-ups
- 75 burpees

DAY 73

Original Session: Warm up - 3 minute assault bike, then 2 rounds of: 10 dislocates, 10 overhead squats, 5 strict press, sumo stretch. Then work to a heavy overhead squat, followed by 4 rounds of 4 overhead squats at 50 percent of maximum effort. Next, at the top of every minute for 9 minutes, complete 4 burpees, 4 thrusters, 4 pull-ups. Finish with 2 rounds of: 10 romanian deadlifts, 10 walking banded lunges, 60 second plank, 10 russian twists.

Home Edition:

- 20 side to side lunges (10 each side)
- 20 frog jumps
- At the top of each minute for 9 minutes, complete: 4 burpees, 4 non-weighted thrusters, 4 push-ups.
- 4 rounds, 30 seconds each: ski abs, plank, russian twists

DAY 74

Original Session: Warm up - 5 minute row, increase speed each minute. Then, work to a heavy back squat. 20 super squats. Finish with 4 rounds of: 500 meter row, 20 second handstand hold, 100 meter kettlebell farmer carry, 100 meter sled pull and drag.

Home Edition:

- 10 minute jog around block, or accumulate 10 minutes of: jogging in place, jumping jacks, jump rope, and/or cardio of choice
- 4 rounds of: 30 second handstand hold, 30 second wall sit, 30 second super man, 30 second hollow hold
- 30-20-10 repetitions of: push-ups, single leg raises, flutter kicks, side plank pulses

DAY 75

The sky is not my limit, I am. — T.F. Hodge

Original Session: Warm up - 2 rounds: 500 meter row, 10 deadlifts, 10 box jumps, 10 walking lunges, pigeon stretch. Then, work to a heavy deadlift. Next, 5 rounds of 5 deadlifts at 80-90 percent of maximum effort. Complete 40-30-20-10 repetitions of wall balls, double unders(120, 90, 60, 30 singles). Finish with as many repetitions as possible of sit ups and plank.

Home Edition:

- 40-30-20-10 repetitions of jump squats and burpees
- Against a 5 minute clock, as many repetitions as possible of sit ups
- Plank hold for time (try to beat your last attempt or hold for 4+ minutes)

DAY 76

Original Session: Warm up - 3 minute assault bike, then 2 rounds of: 5 deadlifts, 5 bent over row, 5 front squat, 5 clean, 5 push press. Then work to a heavy squat clean. Next, every minute on the minute for 6 minutes, complete 1 squat clean at 90% of maximum effort. Finish with 3 rounds for time of: 25 calorie row, 25 sit-ups, 25 burpees, 25 double unders (75 singles).

Home Edition:

- 5 minutes jog around the block, or accumulate 5 minutes of jumping jacks/jogging in place
- 4 rounds: jog around block, (or 4 minutes jog in place) 25 sit-ups, 25 burpees, 25 air squats
- Accumulate 5 minutes total wall sits, handstand holds

DAY 77

Original Session: Warm up - 2 rounds: 250 meter row, 10 back squat, 5 box jumps, pigeon stretch. Complete 3 rounds of: 10 barbell jump squats, 30 second assault bike sprint. Then, 3 rounds of: 10 bench press, 500 meter row. Finish with partner workout: 100 wall balls and 200 kettlebell swings. One partner works while the other partner holds plank until finished.

Home Edition:

- 8 Rounds for Time: 10 push-ups, 10 Air Squats, 10 Burpees, 10 Air Squats
- 1 minute each: plank, side plank elbow taps, (30 seconds each side) sit-ups, mountain climbers, double leg raises, russian twists, superman, hollow hold, standing oblique crunch, single leg raises, sit-ups, flutter kicks, scissor kicks

DAY 78

Original Session: Warm up - Foam roll, pigeon stretch, 5 push press, 5 front squat, 5 squat clean. Work to a heavy clean & jerk. Then, at the top of each minute for 8 minutes, perform one clean & jerk at 70-80% of maximum effort. Finish with 3 rounds of 15 burpee box jumps, 90 second row sprint.

Home Edition:

- 10-9-8-7-6-5-4-3-2-1 Repetitions for time: Burpees, push-ups, sit-ups
- 100 sit-ups

DAY 79

Original Session: "J" Jason Fine Hero Workout. Warm up - 400 meter run, then 2 rounds of: 10 push-ups, 10 air squats, 10 walking lunges. Then, complete 5 rounds of 5 deadlifts at 60% of maximum effort. For time: 400 jump rope buy in, then: 4 rounds of: 10 pull-ups, 10 front squats, 15 push presses, 20 burpees.

Home Edition:

- Run 400 meters (or 4 minutes jumping jacks)
- 50 Air Squats
- Run 400 meters (or 4 minutes jog in place)
- 50 push-ups
- Run 400 meters (or 4 minutes lunges)
- 50 Sit-ups
- Run 400 meters (or 4 minutes air squats)

DAY 80

Original Session: Warm up - 2 rounds: 250 meter row, 10 push-ups, 10 air squats, 5 box jumps, pigeon stretch, instep stretch. 20 super squats. 5 rounds of: 6 sandbag get ups, 6 sandbag cleans, 6 sandbag weighted sprints. Finish with 3 rounds of: 10 toes to bar, 15 box jumps, 20 weighted sit ups.

Home Edition:

- 2 minutes max push-ups
- 1 minute rest
- 2 minutes max sit-ups
- 1 minute rest
- 2 minutes max air squats
- 1 minute rest
- 1 mile run (or 10 minute jog around block)
- 25 v-up sit-ups

DAY 81

Original Session: Warm up - 5 minute assault bike, 5 thrusters, 5 box jumps, pigeon stretch, instep stretch. Work to a heavy thruster. Then, complete 27-21-15-9 calorie row, thrusters.

Home Edition:

- 5 minute jog around your block, or 5 minute jog in place/jumping jacks
- 27-21-15-9 repetitions of: in and out abs, plank-ups, stance jacks, frog jumps, push-ups, tricep dips
- 25 burpees for time

DAY 82

Original Session: Warm up - 400 meter run, then 2 rounds of: 10 air squats, 10 burpees. Then, complete 5 rounds of: 5 pull-ups, 10 ring push-ups. Finish with 23 repetitions each of: deadlifts, push press, back squat, ground to floor.

Home Edition:

- Jog around block for 5 minutes, or 5 minute jog in place
- 4 rounds: 10 air squats, 10 burpees
- 23 repetitions of: Handstand hold seconds, push-ups, single leg raises, side to side hops, butt kickers, high knees, tuck jumps

DAY 83

Original Session: Warm up - 200 meter run, kettlebell swing ladder: 10 each at: 18#, 26#, 35#, 44#, 53#. Complete 3 rounds of: 10 sandbag jump squats, 200 meter sprint. Then finish 3 rounds of: 12 deadlifts, 1 minute burpees. 15 minute prowler relay.

Home Edition:

- Against a 10 minute clock, perform 30 seconds of jump squats, 30 seconds jog in place
- Against a 10 minute clock, 30 seconds burpees, 30 seconds rest
- Max all out mountain climbers for 2 minutes, max sit ups for 2 minutes
- Jog around your block or finish with 5 minutes jumping jacks

DAY 84

Original Session: Warm up - 5 minutes - switch every 15 seconds between push-ups, air squats, mountain climbers, jump squats. 5 rounds of: 5 strict press, 5 pull-ups. As many rounds as possible in 6 minutes: 200 meter run, 12 wall balls, 12 kettlebell swings. 2 minute anterior banded hip stretch, foam roll.

Home Edition:

- 3 rounds, 1 minute each of: push-ups, air squats, mountain climbers, jump squats
- 5 rounds of: 30 second handstand hold, 30 seconds moving push-ups
- As many rounds as possible against a 6 minute clock: 12 frog jumps, 12 jumping lunges, 12 stance jacks
- 100 sit-ups

DAY 85

WHAT HAPPENS TO US ARE TINY MATTERS COMPARED TO OUR RESPONSE TO ANY SITUATION. — LAILAH GIFTY AKITA

Original Session: Warm up - At the top of every minute for 5 minutes: 5 push-ups, 5 air squats, 5 box jumps. Work to a heavy deadlift. Then, at the top of every minute for 10 minutes - even/odd - 5 deadlifts, 10 wall balls. Then, 5 rounds of: 250 meter row for time. Finish with couch stretch and pigeon stretch.

Home Edition:

- 5 rounds of: 5 push-ups, 5 jump squats, 5 burpees
- For 10 minutes, at the top of each even minute, perform 5 diamond jumps, at the top of each odd minute, perform 10 air squats
- 5 rounds of: 2 minute sprint around your block (or 2 minute jog in place)

DAY 86

Original Session: 2 rounds of: 250 meter row, 10 lunges, 10 air squats, 10 kettlebell swings. Work to a heavy back squat, then 3 rounds of 5 back squats at 60%, 70%, 80% of maximum effort. Next, complete 5 rounds of: 20 kettlebell swings, 10 burpees, 1 minute heavy plate overhead carry. Finish with 3 rounds of 10 superman pulses.

Home Edition:

- 2 rounds of: 3 minute jog around your block or 3 minute jog in place, 10 walking lunges, 10 air squats, 10 push-ups.
- 50 air squats
- 50 burpees
- 50 sit-ups

DAY 87

Original Session: Warm up - 4 minutes, 15 seconds each: air squats, mountain climbers, push-ups, jump squats. Work to a heavy high hang clean. Then complete 4 rounds of: 3 high hang cleans at 70% of maximum effort. Finish with 2 rounds of: 800 meter run, 50 wall balls, 25 pull-ups.

Home Edition:

- 4 rounds: 5 air squats, 10 mountain climbers, 5 leg raises or v-up sit-ups, 10 lunges
- 1 mile run (or accumulate 10 minutes of: jumping jacks, jog in place, jump rope, butt kickers, high knees, heisman)
- 100 air squats
- 50 push-ups
- 100 sit-ups

DAY 88

Original Session: Warm up - 3 minute assault bike, then 2 rounds of: 10 PVC dislocates, 5 side lunges each side, 10 air squats. Technique work: back of the neck jerk. 15 minutes of jerk progression/technique. 5 rounds of: 200 meter run, 5 ground to overhead, 10 toes to bar. Finish with 3 rounds of: 8 kettlebell romanian deadlift each leg.

Home Edition:

- 5 rounds: 20 frog jumps, 20 sit-up-v-ups, (or 20 leg raises) 3 minute jog around block or 3 minute jog in place
- 4 rounds: 1 minute each front leg raise pulses right side, leg raise pulses left side
- 20 burpees for time

DAY 89

Original Session: Warm up - 2 minute assault bike, then 2 rounds of: 20 air squats, 15 box jumps, 10 sit-ups. Partner workout: One partner completes a 200 meter run while the other partner works. Switch between: kettlebell swings, sit-ups, burpees, lunges, jump rope, until finished. 2 rounds rope complex: 20 slams, 40 side to sides, 20 jumping jacks. Then complete 3 rounds of plank hold, pigeon stretch, dislocates, foam roll

Home Edition:

- 50 tuck jumps
- 50 push-ups
- 50 air squat
- 50 second handstand hold
- 50 walking lunges
- 50 sit-ups
- 50 second L-sit hold
- 50 Burpees

DAY 90

IF YOU WANT SOMETHING YOU'VE NEVER HAD, YOU MUST BE WILLING TO DO SOMETHING YOU'VE NEVER DONE. — THOMAS JEFFERSON

Original Session: Warm up - 2 rounds: 250 meter row, 10 lunges each side, 10 jumping air squats, 10 kettlebell swings. Work to a heavy back squat. Then, complete 6 rounds of 4 back squats, 100 meter sprint (walk back is rest). Next, 500 meter row followed by 3 rounds of: 15 wall balls, 15 box jumps, 15 kettlebell swings, 1 minute assault bike sprint.

Home Edition:

- 10 rounds: 10 air squats, 1 minute sprint around block or 1 minute sprint in place, 1 minute rest
- 3 rounds: 20 jumping lunges, 10 push-ups, 5 burpees
- 100 sit-ups for time

DAY 91

Original Session: Warm up - 3 minute row, then 2 rounds of: 5 push press, 5 push-ups, 10 lunges, 10 banded side steps. Then, complete 5 rounds (up in weight each round) 5 push press, 5 pull-ups. Next, finish 3 rounds, 1 minute each exercise: row, box jump, wall ball, kettlebell swing, weighted sit-ups. 1 minute rest between movements. 3 rounds of 15 superman pulses.

Home Edition:

- 2 rounds: 20 second handstand hold, 5 push-ups, 10 lunges each side, 10 stance jacks
- 5 rounds: 10 pike push-ups, 20 ski abs
- 10-20-30 repetitions of: burpees, jumping jacks, high knees

DAY 92

> *EVERYONE HAS THE ABILITY TO ACCOMPLISH UNIQUE FEATS, EVERYONE. YOU CHOOSE THIS. BECOME SOMEONE GREAT IN ONE OTHER LIFE. FORGET ABOUT FAILING TOO MANY. WHO CARES? DOESN'T MATTER WHEN YOU START OR FINISH, JUST START, NO DEVIATIONS, NO EXCUSES. —TOM PLATZ*

Original Session: Warm up - 5 minutes 30 seconds on/30 seconds rest assault bike. Work to a heavy deadlift. Next, complete 4 rounds of 3 deadlifts at 70% of maximum effort, followed by a heavy prowler push or sled pull. Finish with 4 rounds of: 400 meter run, 15 burpees, 30 kettlebell swings.

Home Edition:

- 5 minute jog around your block (may jog in place or accumulate 5 minutes cardio of your choice)
- 5 rounds of: 10 push-ups, 1 minute rest, 10 jump squats, 1 minute rest
- 50-40-30-20-10: bicycle crunches, flutter kicks, russian twists, standing oblique crunch (split ½ right ½ left)

DAY 93

Original Session: Warm up - 3 minute assault bike, 10 burpees, 10 lunges, 10 push-ups, 10 air squats, pigeon stretch, instep stretch. Then, complete 3 rounds of: 8 hang power cleans, (up in weight each round) 200 meter run. Next, finish 3 rounds of: 8 back squats, 2 minute row. Finally, complete 15 burpee pull-ups, 20 jump squats, 25 wall balls, 30 calorie row.

Home Edition:

- 5 minute jog around your block or 5 minute jog in place
- 3 rounds: 10 burpees, 10 lunges, 10 push-ups, 10 air squats
- For time: 50 high knees, 50 butt kickers, 50 stance jacks, 50 in and out abs

DAY 94

Original Session: Warm up - 15 seconds each: gym sprints, air squats, push-ups, shoulder mobility. 5 rounds: 3 push press at 70% of maximum effort. Then, with a partner: (one works, one rests) 40 kettlebell swing, 40 calorie assault bike, 30 kettlebell swing, 30 calorie assault bike, 20 kettlebell swing, 20 calorie assault bike, 10 kettlebell swing, 10 calorie assault bike. Finish with 40 strict pull-ups for time with a partner.

Home Edition:

- 1 mile run (may substitute for 100 burpees)
- 40-30-20-10 air squats, high knees
- Accumulate 5 minutes in plank position of your choice

DAY 95

Original Session: Warm up - 2 rounds: 30 second jump rope, 8 front squat, calf smash, t-spine stretch. Complete 6 rounds of 3 front squats. Then, finish 5 rounds of: 400 meter run, 2 minute rest. Finish with 3 rounds of 1 minute plank.

Home Edition:

- 5 minute jump rope (may substitute for jumping jacks)
- 3 rounds, 2 minutes each: squat thrusts, walking lunges, moving push-ups, sit-ups, mountain climbers, heisman, frog jumps
- 5 minute jog around your block or 40 burpees

DAY 96

Original Session: Warm up - 2 rounds: 10/10 step ups, 10 kettlebell swings, 10 deadlifts. Work to a heavy set of 3 deadlifts, no more than 80% of maximum effort. 9, 15, 20 deadlifts, burpees. Finish with 3 rounds of: 15 GHD sit-ups, 30 Russian twists, 20 lateral band walks each side.

Home Edition:

- 20 Rounds for Time:
- 5 push-ups
- 5 air squats
- 5 sit-ups

DAY 97

Original Session: Warm up - At the top of each minute for 5 minutes: 5 push-ups, 5 box jumps, 5 air squats. Then, 6 rounds of: 4 minutes each - 400 meter run, 10 burpee box jumps. Finish with 50 v-ups, superman holds in between.

Home Edition:

- For 20 minutes, at the top of each minute / repeat until 20 minutes is up:
- Minute 1: 15 push-ups
- Minute 2: 10 air squats
- Minute 3: 15 sit-ups
- Minute 4: 20 lunges

DAY 98

Original Session: Warm up - 800 meter run. Overhead squat progression / technique work. Finish with 500 meter row, then 50 kettlebell swing, 50 butterfly sit-up, 40 kettlebell swing, 40 butterfly sit-up, 30 kettlebell swing, 30 butterfly sit-up, 20 kettlebell swing, 20 butterfly sit-up, 10 kettlebell swing, 10 butterfly sit-up. Mobility, foam roll

Home Edition:

- 7 minute jog around your block or accumulate 7 minutes jumping jacks, jump rope, high knees, butt kickers, jogging in place
- 50-40-30-20-10 repetitions of: air squats, sit-ups, push-ups
- 20 burpees

DAY 99

Original Session: Warm up - 5 hang cleans, 5 box jumps, 5 push-ups, 5 toes to bar. Work to a heavy squat clean. Then, at the top of each minute for 8 minutes, 2 hang squat cleans, 2 box jumps. Finish with 5 rounds of: 200 meter run, 30 double unders, (60 singles) 15 wall balls, 9 pull-ups. Foam roll, mobility.

Home Edition:

- 8 rounds of: 3 minute jog around your block or run in place, 30 jumping jacks, 15 jump squats, 9 push-ups
- 1 minute each: v-up sit-ups, standing oblique crunch, hollow hold, superman hold, flutter kicks, bicycle crunches, scissor kicks, double leg raises

DAY 100

Original Session: Warm up - At the top of each minute for 5 minutes: 5 push-ups, 5 box jumps, 5 air squats. Then, work to a heavy deadlift. At the top of each minute for 10 minutes, 5 deadlifts, 10 push-ups, rest. Finish with 5 rounds 250 meter all out row sprints.

Home Edition:

- At the top of each minute for 5 minutes: 5 push-ups, 5 box jumps, 5 air squats
- Every minute for 10 minutes, complete 10 push-ups (remaining time is rest)
- 5 rounds jog around your block or 75 burpees

DAY 101

Original Session: Warm up - 400 meter run, then 2 rounds of: 10 air squats, 5 box jumps, 5 burpees, instep stretch. Work to a heavy hang power clean. Then complete 4 rounds of 3 hang power cleans at 75% of maximum effort. Next, ladder of 10-9-8-7-6-5-4-3-2-1 of the following: walking lunges, kettlebell swings, pull-ups. Finish with accumulating L-sit hold for 3 rounds of 15+ seconds.

Home Edition:

- 3 rounds: 10 air squats, 5 jumping lunges each side, 5 burpees
- 10-9-8-7-6-5-4-3-2-1 repetitions of: air squats, push-ups, v-up sit-ups, side lunges (each side)
- 4 rounds: 20 tricep dips, 20 flutter kicks

DAY 102

> *PEOPLE LAUGH AND CALL ME LAZY, WHILE THEY TWIT AROUND IN THEIR THREE-HOUR WORKOUT MAKING ZERO PROGRESS. SOMETIMES, INSTEAD OF WHAT YOU DO IN THE WEIGHT ROOM, IT'S WHAT YOU DON'T DO THAT WILL LEAD TO SUCCESS. — JIM WENDLER*

Original Session: Warm up - 30 seconds each for 3 rounds: assault bike, air squat, push-ups. Then, 3 rounds of: 10 jump squats, 200 meter run. Next, 3 rounds of: 10 dumbbell push press, 1 minute jump rope. Finish with a prowler relay until the coach says we're done.

Home Edition:

- For time, complete 1,500 repetitions
- Choose from the following pool of movements:
- Air squats, superman holds, hollow holds, burpees, jumping jacks, lunges, pistol squats, push-ups, sit-ups, mountain climbers, wall sit pulses

DAY 103

Original Session: Warm up - 4 minute assault bike, 4-5 minute hip and ankle mobility work. Work to 70% of maximum effort deadlift, then complete 5 rounds of 5 deadlifts at that weight. Finally, 4 rounds of: 30 wall balls, 200 meter run.

Home Edition:

- 5 minute jog around your block or accumulate 5 minutes of: jumping jacks, high knees, butt kickers, heisman
- 4 rounds: 30 seconds each: Wall sits, handstand holds
- 4 rounds: 30 air squats, 3 minute jog around block or 3 minutes jog in place

DAY 104

Original Session: Warm up - 2 rounds: 10 banded side steps each leg, 10 air squats, 10 box jumps, 10 push-ups. Then complete the following movements in a 10-9-8-7-6-5-4-3-2-1 ladder: pull-ups, push-ups (add 2 for push-ups). Next, 4 rounds of: 10 hang squat cleans, 15 burpees, 200 meter run, 1 minute rest. Finish with 1 minute maximum assault bike and foam roll/couch stretch.

Home Edition:

- 4 rounds: 10 reclining marching glute bridge each side, 10 air squats, 10 speed skaters each side, 10 push ups
- 10-9-8-7-6-5-4-3-2-1 ladder of: spiderman mountain climbers, sit-ups
- 4 rounds: 10 air squats, 3 minute jog around block or 3 minutes jumping jacks

DAY 105

Original Session: Warm up - Double under practice, then work to heavy front squat. 5 rounds: 2 front squat at 80% of maximum effort, 2 high box jumps. Then, complete 50-40-30-20-10 double unders (3x singles) and butterfly sit-ups. Finish with 3 rounds of: 15 GHD hip extensions or superman holds.

Home Edition:

- 7 minute jog around your block or 7 minutes jump rope, jumping jacks, jog in place
- 50-40-30-20-10 air squats, sit-ups
- Tabata abs: 8 rounds: 20 seconds superman hold, 10 seconds rest, 20 seconds plank, 10 seconds rest

DAY 106

Original Session: Warm up - 5 deadlifts, 5 box jumps, 10 walking lunges, 2 rounds of: 1 minute step ups. 3 rounds of 8 deadlifts, 4 box jumps, 400 meter run, (up in weight and height each round) 1:30 rest. Then, complete 40-30-20-10 wall balls, burpees (½ repetitions for burpees).

Home Edition:

- 100 burpees
- 100 sit-ups
- 100 walking toe touches

DAY 107

Original Session: Warm up - 200 meter run, 10 banded air squats, 10 dislocates, 10 push presses. Then, work to a heavy barbell complex of: strict press, push press, push jerk. Complete 5 rounds of the above complex at a manageable weight for all movements. Next, 3 minute maximum effort row, rest 2 minutes. Then, 2 minutes chest to bar pull-ups, rest 2 minutes. Finish with 1 minute maximum burpees.

Home Edition:

- 5 minute jog around your block or accumulate 5 minutes jumping jacks, high knees, and butt kickers.
- 3 rounds: 10 lunges each side, 10 air squats, 10 push-ups
- 10 minutes maximum effort burpees

DAY 108

Original Session: Warm up - 2 rounds: 8 front squats, 8 push-ups, 8 sit-ups, sumo wall sits. Work to a heavy front squat with a 3 second pause at the bottom (2 front squats). Then, complete 4 rounds of this complex at 90% of maximum effort. Next, 4 rounds of: 20 calorie assault bike or row, 10 squat cleans from the floor to a thruster (clusters). Finish with 3 rounds of 5 negative tricep dips.

Home Edition:

- 2 rounds: 8 jumping lunges each side, 8 air squats, 8 push-ups, 8 sit-ups, 30 second wall sit hold
- 5 rounds: 20 reverse lunges, (10 each side) 20 calf raises, 20 glute bridge walk-outs, (may substitute glute bridge raises) 20 reclining side leg raises each side, 20 air squats
- 1 minute tricep dips

DAY 109

Original Session: Warm up - 3 minute assault bike, 2 rounds of barbell complex (back squat, push press, front squat, deadlift). Work to a heavy power clean. Then, at the top of every minute for 10 minutes: 2 power cleans, 5 push-ups. For time: 20 calorie row, 20 back squats, 20 burpee box jumps, 20 wall balls, 20 push presses, 20 calorie row.

Home Edition:

- 5 minute jog around your block (or accumulate 5 minutes of: jogging in place, jump rope, jumping jacks, high knees, heisman)
- For 10 minutes, at the top of each minute complete: 2 jump squats, 5 push-ups
- 20 jumping jacks, 20 air squats, 20 burpees, 20 lunges each side, 20 push-ups, 20 sit-ups, 20 jumping jacks

DAY 110

> *DID YOU EVER NOTICE THOSE WHO CRITICIZE THE STRONG OR THE ELITE ARE USUALLY WEAKER OR LESS SUCCESSFUL THAN THOSE THEY PASS JUDGMENT ON. AND THOSE WHO ARE STRONG OR ELITE IN THEIR RESPECTIVE SPORTS RARELY CONDEMN THOSE WHO ARE NOT AS STRONG OR AS SUCCESSFUL AS THEY ARE. — LOUIE SIMMONS*

Original Session: Warm up - 2 rounds: 1 minute assault bike, 5 deadlifts, 5 box jumps, 5 push-ups, 5 air squats, dislocates, sumo. Work to a heavy 1 rep maximum deadlift. Then, 3 rounds of 3 deadlifts, up in weight each round. Finish with 5 rounds of 3 minutes, as many repetitions as possible: 3 hang cleans, 6 push-ups, 9 air squats.

Home Edition:

- At the top of every minute for 30 minutes:
- 5 burpees, 9 v-up sit-ups, 12 lunges (6 each side)

DAY 111

Original Session: Warm up - 250 meter row, 10 push-ups, 10 air squats, 10 lunges each side, dislocates, sumo. Work to a heavy hang clean. Then perform 6 rounds of 1 hang clean at 90% of maximum effort. Complete 4 rounds of: 400 meter run, 10 pull-ups, 8 burpee box jumps

Home Edition:

- 2 rounds: 3 minute jog around your block, (or jog in place) 10 push-ups, 10 air squats, 10 side lunges
- 4 rounds: 30 second handstand holds (may substitute for wall walks)
- 4 rounds: 3-5 minute jog around your block, (may substitute 100 jumping jacks) 10 flutter kicks, 8 burpees

DAY 112

Original Session: Warm up - 400 meter run, then 2 rounds of: 8 lunges each side, 8 lateral band walks each side, 8 strict presses, pigeon stretch. Then, 3 rounds of: 10 strict presses, 500 meter row, rest 2 minutes. Next, 3 rounds of: 10 sandbag jump squats, 200 meter sprint. Finish with 4 rounds of a heavy prowler push, down to the end of the gym and back.

Home Edition:

- 50 jumping jacks, 50 high knees, 50 butt kickers, 50 side to side jumps
- 2 rounds: 20 squat position side steps, (10 each side) 20 push-ups, 20 jump squats, 3 minute sprint around your block (may substitute 3 minute sprint in place)
- 1 minute each of the following: bicycle sit ups, plank, hollow extension to cannon ball, bird dogs, side plank pulses, (30 seconds each side) scissor kicks, standing oblique crunch (30 seconds each side)

DAY 113

Original Session: Warm up - 10 lunges each side, 5 box jumps, 5 overhead squats, 5 pull-ups. 3-6-9-12-15 repetitions of: deadlifts, push-ups, wall balls. In between each set, 200 meter run. Then complete a partner 1,000 meter row.

Home Edition:

- 3 rounds of: 10 side lunges each side, 5 jump squats, 5 push-ups
- 3-6-9-12-15 repetitions of: burpees, broad jumps, moving plank (for plank, repetitions are in each direction - 6-9-24-30 total)
- 10 minute jog around block or accumulate 10 minutes of jumping jacks, jump rope, switch kicks, overhead air squats

DAY 114

Original Session: Warm up - 2 rounds: 1 minute assault bike, 5 box jumps, 10 sumo lunges, 5 kettlebell swings, pigeon stretch, instep stretch. Then, complete 3 rounds of: 5 left 5 right barbell rack lunges, 5 box jumps, 400 meter run, 90 seconds rest. Next, 3 rounds: 8 hang power snatches, 300 meter row, 60 seconds rest. Finally, 3 rounds: 25 butterfly sit-ups, 25 wall balls.

Home Edition:

- 2 rounds: 1 minute jumping jacks, 10 air squats, 10 lunges, (5 right, 5 left) 10 push-ups
- 3 rounds: 1 minute each movement: jumping lunges, air squats, high knees
- 10-20-30-40-50 repetitions of: burpees, sit-ups

DAY 115

Original Session: Warm up - 30 seconds on/30 seconds off assault bike, (5 minutes) dislocates, sumo stretch. At the top of each minute for 24 minutes, complete 15-20 push-ups. Then, 21-15-9 of: thrusters, pull-ups, 200 meter run between sets. Foam roll, couch stretch.

Home Edition:

- 3 minutes jog around your block or accumulate 3 minutes of jumping jacks, heisman, butt kickers
- At the top of every minute for 24 minutes, perform 15-20 push-ups (or variation for scaling)
- 21-15-9 repetitions of: jump squats, mountain climbers, tricep dips

DAY 116

Original Session: Warm up - 2 rounds: 200 meter run, 10 kettlebell swings, 15 air squats, 5 pull-ups. For time: 400 meter run, 10 pull-ups, 20 kettlebell swings, 30 box jumps, 40 push-ups, 60 burpees, 400 meter run. FInish with core work of choice and foam roll.

Home Edition:

- 4 minute jog around your block, (or 4 minutes jumping jacks) 10 tricep dips, 20 mountain climbers, 30 air squats, 40 push-ups, 60 burpees, 4 minute jog around your block or 4 minute high knees.
- Abdominal circuit: 1 minute each: superman hold, hollow hold, elevated side plank, (30 seconds each side) front plank, flutter kicks, sit-ups, standing oblique crunch (30 seconds each side)

DAY 117

Original Session: Warm up - 3 minute assault bike, then 2 rounds barbell complex (5 repetitions each: deadlift, row, hang power clean, front squat, push press, back squat). Pigeon stretch, instep stretch. Work to a heavy back squat. Then, complete 4 rounds of: 5 back squat at 80% of maximum effort. Next, against a 4 minute clock: 500 meter row, finish with burpee pull-ups. Against another 4 minute clock, 500 meter row, finish with box jumps. Last, complete 400 meter run for time.

Home Edition:

- 100 burpees
- 100 sit-ups
- 100 air squats

DAY 118

Original Session: Warm up - 500 meter row, then 2 rounds of: 5 lunges, 10 GHD sit-ups, 5 deadlifts, instep stretch. Perform the following repetitions of deadlifts: 5-5-3-3-1-1 increasing in weight to 90% of maximum effort. Then as many rounds as possible in 20 minutes of: 5 pull-ups, 10 push-ups, 15 air squats. Every 4th round, run 400 meters. Finish with 3 rounds of 10 GHD sit-ups.

Home Edition:

- 3 rounds of: 10 lunges, 10 sit-ups, 10 burpees
- Against a 20 minute clock, perform as many rounds as possible of: 5 tricep dips, 10 push-ups, 15 air squats. Every 4th round, stop and do 50 jumping jacks or complete a 4 minute jog around your block

DAY 119

Original Session: Warm up - 1 mile jog. Then, 7 rounds of: 7 push-ups, 7 squats, 7 sit-ups, 7 burpees, 7 lunges, 7 tricep extensions, 7 russian twists. Finish with 1 mile run.

Home Edition:

- 1 mile run (may substitute for accumulating 8 minutes of: jumping jacks, high knees, butt kickers, heisman)
- 7 rounds of: 7 push-ups, 7 squats, 7 sit-ups, 7 burpees, 7 lunges, 7 tricep dips, 7 russian twists.
- Finish with 1 mile run (may substitute for accumulating 8 minutes of: jumping jacks, high knees, butt kickers, heisman)

DAY 120

Original Session: Warm up - 400 meter run, then 4 rounds of: 15 each: lunges, air squats, swinging pull-ups, pull-ups. Then, 9 rounds: deadlift, hang clean, clean. Partner: 20 wall balls, 20 pull-ups, 20 push presses, 20 kettlebell swings. Unbroken: 20 front squats, 20 wall balls. Finish with superman, v-sit-ups, shoulder stretch.

Home Edition:

- 4 minute jog around your block (or 4 minutes jumping jacks)
- 4 rounds: 20 repetitions each: lunges, (10 right/10 left) mountain climbers, air squats
- Against a 20 minute clock, as many rounds as possible of: 20 repetitions each: jumping squats, side to side lunges, push-ups
- Abdominal circuit: 1 minute each - hollow hold to cannon ball crunch, front plank, elevated side plank, (30 seconds each side) flutter kicks, bicycle crunches, superman hold, standing oblique crunch (30 seconds each side)

DAY 121

> *ENDURANCE PRECEDES SUCCESS. — WAYNE CHIRISA*

Original Session: Warm up - 400 meter run, then 2 rounds of: 10 air squats, 5 jump squats, 10 kettlebell swings, pigeon stretch, instep stretch. 3 rounds: 12 barbell jump squats, 500 meter row. Then 3 rounds: 12 walking lunges each side, 100 meter sprint, walk back is rest. For time: 12-9-6-3: burpee pull-ups, American style kettlebell swing.

Home Edition:

- Buy in: 30 burpees
- 4-8-12-16-20-24-28-32-36-40 repetitions of: lunges each side, plank shoulder taps
- 40-36-32-28-24-20-16-12-8-4 repetitions of: floor switch kicks, stance jacks
- Buy out: 30 burpees

DAY 122

Original Session: Warm up - 500 meter row, then 2 rounds of: 10 lunges each side, 10 kettlebell swings, 10 sit-ups, 5 deadlift, pigeon stretch. Work to maximum effort deadlift. As many rounds as possible in 9 minutes: 15 deadlift, 200 meter run. 3 rounds: 10 bent over row, 10 left/10 right single leg glute bridge, 15 weighted sit-ups.

Home Edition:

- 2 rounds: 4 minute jog around your block or 4 minutes jumping jacks, 10 lunges each side, 10 air squats, 10 sit-ups
- As many rounds as possible in 9 minutes: 20 wall sit pulses, 3 minute run around your block or 75 high knees
- 3 rounds: 10 tricep dips, 10 left/10 right single leg glute bridge pulses, 15 sit-ups

DAY 123

Original Session: Warm up - 5 minutes: 30 seconds on, 30 seconds off assault bike, mobility, foam roll. 5 rounds: 3 deadlifts, (up in weight each round) 2 box jumps. 5 rounds, 3 minutes each - 200 meter run, use remaining time for as many rounds as possible of: 5 pull-ups, 10 push-ups, 15 air squats. 90 seconds rest between rounds.

Home Edition:

- 5 minutes: 30 seconds high knees, 30 seconds jog in place
- 5 rounds: 3 wall walks or 30 second handstand hold, 10 tuck jumps
- 5 rounds, against a 3 minute clock: 2 minute sprint in place, use remaining time for as many rounds as possible of: 5 push-ups, 10 sit-ups, 15 air squats. 90 seconds rest between rounds

DAY 124

Original Session: Warm up - 500 meter row, snatch warm up with PVC. 3 rounds: 6 hang power snatch, 500 meter row, 2 minute rest. 3 rounds: 10 back squats, 2 minutes 40 seconds on/20 seconds off assault bike, 2 minutes rest. Maximum unbroken wall balls.

Home Edition:

- Against a 24 minute clock, as many rounds as possible of the following:
- 24 jumping lunges, 24 hollow rocks, 24 air squats, 24 burpees
- 50 butterfly sit-ups

DAY 125

Original Session: Warm up - 5 minute assault bike, mobility. Work to heavy power clean, push press. Then, complete 3-6-9-12-15 repetitions of pull-ups, power clean/push press complex.

Home Edition:

- 1 mile run (may substitute for 10 minutes of 1 minute each: jumping jacks, high knees, butt kickers, heisman, frog jumps)
- 4-8-12-16-20 repetitions of: moving push-ups, glute bridge walk outs
- 40 bicycle crunches

DAY 126

Original Session: Warm up - 10 lunges each side, 10 push-ups, 10 kettlebell swings, dislocates, instep stretch. With a partner, complete: 1,000 meter row, 50 squat cleans, 200 meter run, 50 box jumps, 200 meter run, 50 pull-ups, 200 meter run, 50 back squats, 1,000 meter row.

Home Edition:

- 100 jumping jacks
- 20 burpees, 20 jumping lunges
- 20 burpees, 20 push-ups
- 20 burpees, jump squats
- 100 jumping jacks

DAY 127

Original Session: Warm up - 2 rounds: 1 minute assault bike, 10 lunges each side, 10 box jumps, 10 kettlebell swings, dislocate and pigeon stretch. Work to a heavy squat clean. Then, 5 rounds of: 5 cleans at 70% of maximum effort, 400 meter run, 2 minutes rest. Prowler sprint relay.

Home Edition:

- 4 rounds: 1 minute jumping jacks, 10 lunges each side, 10 squat jumps, 10 push-ups
- 50-40-30-20-10 repetitions of: burpees, sit-ups

DAY 128

> *WHEN THE RUSSIAN KETTLEBELL MEETS AN AMERICAN STEAK, IT IS A BEAUTIFUL THING. — PAVEL TSATSOULINE*

Original Session: Warm up - 2 rounds: 200 meter run, 10 lunges each side, 10 kettlebell swings, 10 push presses. Work to a heavy push press. Then, complete 5 rounds of: 3 push presses, 15 push-ups. Next, 3 rounds of: 50 air squats, 14 pull-ups, 10 power cleans. Finish with 3 rounds of: 1 minute plank, 20 Russian twists.

Home Edition:

- 5 minute jog around your block, or accumulate 5 minutes of: jumping jacks, jog in place, butt kickers, high knees
- 5 rounds: 30 second handstand hold, (may substitute for plank) 10 push-ups
- 3 rounds: 50 air squats, 20 mountain climbers
- 3 rounds: 1 minute each: plank, unweighted Russian twists

DAY 129

Original Session: Warm up - 4 rounds, 15 seconds each: air squat, push-up, plank, rest. pull-ups complex: 5 rounds: 3 negatives, 3 partner assisted, 3 jumping. Then, for 10 minutes, as many rounds as possible: 5 thrusters, 5 box jumps, 10 thrusters, 10 box jumps (increase by 5 each time). 3 rounds: 10 GHD sit-ups, 10 GHD hip extensions.

Home Edition:

- 4 rounds: 15 seconds each: air squats, push-ups, plank, rest
- 5 rounds: max handstand holds (try for at least 20 seconds each round)
- Against a 10 minute clock, as many rounds as possible of: 5 push-ups, 5 air squats, 10 push-ups, 10 air squats (increase by 5 repetitions each time)
- 50 sit-ups, 50 glute bridge raises

DAY 130

Original Session: Warm up - 2 rounds: 30 second assault bike, 8 back squats, 10 banded walks each side, pigeon/instep stretch. 5 rounds: 8 back squats. Then 5 rounds for time: 50 double unders, (or 150 singles) 10 toes to bar, 16 gym length farmers carry. Finish with 3 rounds of 1:00 plank hold.

Home Edition:

- 5 minute jog around your block, or 25 burpees
- 5 rounds: 50 jumping jacks, 10 v-sit-ups, 10 moving push-ups
- 3 rounds: 1 minute plank hold of choice

DAY 131

WHEN PEOPLE TELL YOU THAT YOU AREN'T SOMETHING OR YOU CAN'T ACCOMPLISH YOUR DREAMS, YOU CAN EITHER CRY ABOUT IT OR PROVE THEM WRONG. — IMANIA MARGRIA

Original Session: Warm up - 2 rounds: 5 deadlifts, 5 box jumps, 5 lunges each side, dislocates, instep. 100 calorie assault bike. Then, 3 rounds of: 20 deadlifts, 20 bar facing burpees. Finish with 3 rounds of: 10 squat cleans, 400 meter run.

Home Edition:

- 10 air squats, 10 lunges each side, 10 push-ups
- 10 minute run around your block, (may substitute for 3 250mping jacks)
- 3 rounds: 20 air squats, 20 burpees
- 3 rounds: 10 floor switch kicks, 3 minute high knees or jog in place

DAY 132

Original Session: Warm up - 2 rounds: 10 air squats, 10 kettlebell swings, 10 box jumps, sumo stretch, dislocates. Work to a starting working weight front squat. Then, 6 rounds: 3 front squats, (up in weight each round) 1 heavy prowler push. Next, complete 5 rounds of: 200 meter run, 10 kettlebell swings, 10 pull-ups, 10 kettlebell swings.

Home Edition:

- 1500 repetitions of your choice of movements: Air squats, burpees, back extensions, jumping jacks, lunges, pistol squats, push-ups, sit-ups, oblique crunch, high knees, jumping lunges

DAY 133

Original Session: Warm up - 2 rounds: 30 second jump rope, 10 air squats, 10 banded walk each side, 10 push-ups, instep stretch. 6 rounds of 3 deadlifts up in weight each round. Then, with a partner (one works while other rests) Row: 500 meter, 400 meter, 300 meter, 200 meter, 100 meter. Wall balls (2x) 30, 20, 10.

Home Edition:

- 2 rounds: 30 seconds jumping jacks, 10 air squats, 10 lateral lunges each side, 10 push-ups.
- 4 rounds of 10 single leg deadlifts each leg
- Alternate between the following: (may substitute for running in place) 5 minute run, 50 air squats, 4 minute run, 40 sit-ups, 3 minute run, 30 air squats, 2 minute run, 20 sit-ups

DAY 134

Original Session: Warm up - 2 rounds: 1 minute assault bike, 10 banded lunges each side, 10 air squats, instep stretch, dislocates. Work to a heavy deadlift. Then, 8 rounds (every 2 minutes) 10 deadlifts, 10 toes to bar. Finish with 750 meter row for time.

Home Edition:

- 8 rounds: 10 push-ups, 10 double leg raises
- 10 minute jog around your block or 50 air squats and 50 burpees

DAY 135

Original Session: Warm up - 3 minute assault bike, then 2 rounds: 5 lunges each side, 5 ring rows, 5 push-ups, dislocates. Work to a heavy set of 10 bench presses. 4 rounds: 10 bench press, 10 ring rows. 5 rounds: 8 back squats, 4 jump squats with sandbag, 4 jump squats without sandbag, 100 meter sprint, walk back is rest. 3 rounds: 30 seconds ea: push-ups, plank, rest.

Home Edition:

- 3 minute jog around your block or 3 minute jumping jacks, 5 lateral lunges each side, 5 tricep dips, 5 push-ups.
- 4 rounds: 10 push-ups, 10 tricep dips
- 5 rounds: 8 air squats, 8 jump squats, 1 minute sprint in place
- 3 rounds: 30 seconds front plank, 30 seconds side plank each side

DAY 136

Original Session: Warm up - 2 rounds: 30 seconds jump rope, 30 seconds lunges, 30 seconds plank, 30 seconds rest. 10 rounds of: 2 squat cleans up in weight each round. At the top of each minute for 7 minutes: 7 thrusters, 7 burpees. 3 rounds: 15 GHD sit ups, 15 GHD hip extensions.

Home Edition:

- 2 rounds: 30 seconds high knees, 30 seconds reverse lunges, 30 seconds plank, 30 seconds rest
- 10 rounds: 10 jump squats
- At the top of each minute for 7 minutes, perform 7 burpees, 7 sit-i[s
- 4 rounds, 1 minute each: superman hold, hollow hold

DAY 137

Original Session: Warm up - 2 rounds: 5 deadlifts, 5 box jumps, 5 lunges each side, dislocates, instep stretch. Work to a heavy deadlift. Then, 3 rounds of: 5 deadlifts at 60% of that effort. Next, 4 rounds against a 3 minute clock: 200 meter run, 10 thrusters, 10 toes to bar, 1 minute rest. Finish with mobility work.

Home Edition:

- 5 rounds: 10 jump squats, 10 lunges each side, 10 push-ups
- 4 rounds against a 3 minute clock: 3 minute jog around your block (or 3 minutes jumping jacks) 10 unweighted squat thrusters, 10 burpees
- Abdominal circuit - 1 minute each: Single leg raises ,(30 seconds each side) butterfly sit-ups, plank, flutter kicks, side plank pulses, (30 seconds each side) hollow hold, superman hold

DAY 138

Original Session: Warm up - At the top of each minute for 5 minutes, complete: 5 push-ups, 5 air squats, one gym length sprint. Work to a heavy front squat. Then, complete 3 rounds of: 5 front squats at 60% of maximum effort, 5 box jumps, 2 minute assault bike sprint, 90 seconds rest. Next, with a partner holding (2) 16k kettlebells in front rack while the other person works, complete: 3 rounds of a 250 meter row.

Home Edition:

- 5 minutes, at the top of each minute: 5 push-ups, 5 air squats, 10 jumping jacks
- 150 air squats
- 3 rounds: 20 mountain climbers, 20 v-sit-ups, 20 side to side lunges each side

DAY 139

Original Session: Warm up - 2 rounds: 200 meter run, 5 hang power cleans, 5 box jumps, 10 push-ups, 10 air squats, dislocates, instep stretch. 5 rounds: as many repetitions as possible in 3 minutes: 3 hang power cleans, 6 push-ups, 9 air squats. Finish with a 15 minute prowler relay.

Home Edition:

- 5 minute jog around your block or 5 minutes jog in place
- 2 rounds: 5 jump squats, 10 push-ups, 10 air squats
- 5 rounds, each against a 3 minute clock: 3 overhead squats, 6 pike push-ups, 9 low squat pulses
- 4 rounds: 30 second handstand holds (may substitute for 2-3 wall walks)

DAY 140

> *EPIC THINGS START WITH SMALL HUMBLE STEPS. PAY RESPECT TO YOUR BEGINNINGS. AND IF YOU'RE JUST STARTING OUT, KNOW THAT IT'S OK TO BE SUCKY. TO BE SMALL. TO BE MESSY AND CHAOTIC. JUST MAKE SURE TO NEVER STOP DREAMING. — VISHEN LAKHIANI*

Original Session: Warm up - 4 minute assault bike, 1 barbell complex (deadlift, row, power clean, front squat, push press). Work to a heavy hang power clean. Then, complete 5 rounds of: 2 power cleans at 80% of maximum effort. 2-4-6-8-10 = front squat, burpee box jump (no rack). 10-8-6-4-2 = shoulder to overhead, chest to bar (no rack).

Home Edition:

- 4 minute jog around your block, or 2 minutes jumping jacks/2 minute jog in place
- 2-4-6-8-10 repetitions of: jump squats, burpees
- 10-8-6-4-2 repetitions of: moving push-ups, plank jacks
- 5 minute maximum effort sit-ups

DAY 141

Original Session: Warm up - 2 rounds: 1 minute row, 1 minute jump rope, 10 push-ups, pigeon stretch, dislocates. 6 rounds: 5 bench press, 3 explosive push-ups. For time: 800 meter run, 30 GHD sit-ups, 30 kettlebell swings, 400 meter run, 20 GHD sit-ups, 20 kettlebell swings, 200 meter run, 10 GHD sit-ups, 10 kettlebell swings. 3 rounds: 10 banded side walks each side.

Home Edition:

- 2 rounds: 1 minute mountain climbers, 1 minute jumping jacks, 5 sit-ups, 5 push-ups
- 6 rounds: 30 second handstand hold, 3 explosive push-ups
- 5 minute jog around your block, or 5 minute run in place, 30 sit-ups, 30 air squats, 4 minute jog around your block or 4 minute run in place, 20 sit-ups, 20 air squats, 3 minute jog around your block or 3 minute run in place, 10 sit-ups, 10 air squats
- 3 rounds: 10 lateral lunges each side

DAY 142

Original Session: Warm up - 2 minutes assault bike, 5 lunges each side, 5 deadlifts, 5 pull-ups, dislocates. 3 rounds: 10 deadlifts up in weight each round, 2 minute row, 90 second rest. 3 rounds: 10 sandbag front squats, 200 meter run, 1 minute rest. 3 rounds: 10 GHD back extensions, 12/12 Russian twists, 8 ring rows, 8 push-ups.

Home Edition:

- 2 minute jumping jacks, 5 lunges each side, 5 plank shoulder taps each side, 10 push-ups
- 3 rounds: 10 moving plank each side, 2 minute jog around your block or run in place
- 3 rounds: 10 frog jumps, 10 switch kicks, 2 minute jog around your block or 2 minutes high knees
- 3 rounds: 12/12 russian twists, 8 tricep dips, 8 push-ups

DAY 143

MAKE EACH DAY YOUR MASTERPIECE. — JOHN WOODEN

Original Session: Warm up - 5 minutes 30 seconds on/30 seconds off assault bike. Split jerk progression: dip, press, eyeball press, jerk. Work to a heavy split jerk, then 5 rounds of 1 split jerk at a working weight. As many rounds as possible in 14 minutes of: 25 calorie row, 25 wall balls, 25 double unders (75 singles)

Home Edition:

- 5 minutes: 30 seconds jumping jacks, 30 seconds jog in place
- For 20 minutes, complete as many rounds as possible of: 25 burpees, 25 sit-ups, 25 air squats

DAY 144

Original Session: Warm up - 3 minutes row, 2 rounds of: 8 lunges each side, 10 sit-ups, 10 push-ups, dislocates, instep stretch. 5 rounds: 8 kettlebell overhead lunges each side. Then, with a partner: 30-20-10 each of kettlebell swings, calorie row, 50 wall balls. Every 2:30, stop and run 200 meters

Home Edition:

- 1 minute each: jog in place, high knees, butt kickers
- 20 lunges each side, 20 push-ups
- 50-40-30-20-10 repetitions of: air squats, sit-ups. Every 3 minutes, stop and complete 3 burpees

DAY 145

Original Session: Warm up - 2 rounds - barbell complex (3 each of: deadlift, power clean, front squat, push press, back squat). Then, complete 5 rounds of: 3 deadlifts up in weight each round until 60 percent of maximum effort is met. Next, complete 4 rounds of: 10 air squats, 10 push-ups. Then, 30 ground to overhead. Finish with 4 rounds of 10 air squats, 10 push-ups.

Home Edition:

- 5 rounds: 1 minute wall squat hold
- 4 rounds: 10 air squats, 10 push-ups
- 30 burpees
- 4 rounds: 10 air squats, 10 push-ups

DAY 146

Original Session: Warm up - 2 rounds: 10 kettlebell swings, 5 box jumps, 10 air squats, 5 jumping pull-ups, sumo stretch, dislocates. 3 rounds: 8 power cleans up in weight each round, 400 meter run. Then, 3 rounds: 20 kettlebell swings, 3 high box jumps, 2 minute row (30 sec fast/30 sec moderate). For time: 20 wall balls, 5 burpees, 20 wall balls, 5 toes to bar, 20 wall balls, 5 burpees, 20 wall balls, 5 toes to bar.

Home Edition:

- 3 rounds: 10 jump squats, 10 butt kickers, 2 minute jog in place
- 3 rounds: 20 mountain climbers, 8 jumping lunges each side
- 20 air squats, 5 burpees, 20 air squats, 5 double leg raises, 20 air squats, 5 burpees, 20 air squats, 5 double leg raises

DAY 147

Original Session: Warm up - 5 minutes: 30 seconds fast 30 seconds moderate assault bike, dislocates, instep stretch. Then, review overhead squat and snatch progression. 6 rounds: 2 snatches. Then, 10 minutes as many rounds as possible: 40 air squats, 30 butterfly sit-ups, 20 double unders (60 singles) 10 push-ups.

Home Edition:

- 5 minute jog around your block, or accumulate 5 minutes of: jumping jacks, high knees, butt kickers
- 6 rounds: maximum squat hold (or chair pose for added difficulty)
- Against a 10 minute clock, as many rounds as possible of: 40 air squats, 30 butterfly sit-ups, 60 jump rope (or jump in place)

DAY 148

Original Session: Warm up - 5 minute assault bike. Then, 3 rounds of: 10 deadlifts up in weight each round, 400 meter run, 90 seconds rest between rounds. 3 rounds: 10 double kettlebell front squats, 2 minute row. Finish with 4 rounds: 8 strict pull-ups, 8 tricep dips, 8 push-ups, 8 GHD sit-ups (30 seconds rest between each round).

Home Edition:

- 5 minute jog around your block or 5 minutes jog in place
- 3 rounds: 1 minute plank hold, 2 minute jog around your block or 2 minutes jumping jacks
- 3 rounds: 10 jump squats, 1 minute jumping jacks
- 4 rounds: 8 switch kicks, 8 tricep dips, 8 walking push-ups, 8 v-sit-ups

DAY 149

> *NO MATTER HOW SICK YOU ARE, NO MATTER WHAT CURRENT STRAINS AND PAINS YOU HAVE, WHEN IT'S IN YOUR BLOOD YOUR ONLY CONCERN IS TO FIND A WAY TO ENTER THE GYM AND CRUSH IRON. — STEVE SHAW*

Original Session: Warm up - 2 rounds: 250 meter row, 10 lunges each side, 10 push-ups, 10 kettlebell swings, dislocates, instep stretch. Work to a heavy hang squat clean. Then 8 rounds, every minute on the minute: 1 hang squat clean, 1 squat clean. Next, 12 minutes, as many rounds as possible of: 15 wall balls, 12 toes to bar, 9 overhead squats.

Home Edition:

- 2 rounds: 2 minute jumping jacks, 10 lunges each side, 10 push-ups, 10 air squats
- At the top of each minute for 8 minutes: 3 burpees, 3 in and out abs
- Against a 12 minute clock, as many rounds of the following as possible: 15 air squats, 12 v-up sit-ups, 9 plank hold shoulder taps

DAY 150

Original Session: Warm up - 2 minute assault bike, then 2 rounds of: 5 front squats, 5 push presses, 5 box jumps, sump stretch, dislocates. 3 rounds: 8 front squat up in weight each round, 30/30 twice though assault bike (fast/moderate). Then, 3 rounds of: 8 bent over rows, 8 push-ups, 90 seconds gym sprints. Finish with a 1,000 meter row for time.

Home Edition:

- 2 minute jog in place, then 2 rounds: 5 air squats, 5 push-ups, 5 jump squats
- 3 rounds: 8 jumping lunges each side, 3 minute sprint around block or 3 minute sprint in place
- 3 rounds: 10 tricep dips, 10 push-ups, 20 heismans
- Finish with 100 burpees for time

DAY 151

HOW DO YOU ACHIEVE EXCELLENCE? 1. MINDSET 2. DISCIPLINE 3. COMMITMENT 4. CONSISTENCY. — BOBBY F. KIMBROUGH, JR.

Original Session: Warm up - 30 seconds on, 30 seconds off assault bike for 5 minutes. 2 rounds: 5 back squats, 5 box jumps, 5 jumping pull-ups, instep stretch. Work to a heavy back squat. Then, 3 rounds of: 2 back squats at 80-90% of maximum effort. Then, pick your poison: 150 wall balls, 75 thrusters, or 30 ground to overheads.

Home Edition:

- 3 minute jog in place, 2 rounds of: 5 air squats, 5 jump squats, 5 push-ups.
- Your choice of: 1 mile run, 300 jumping jacks, 200 sit-ups, or 100 push-ups

DAY 152

Original Session: Warm up - 3 minute row, then 2 rounds: 5 lunges each side, 10 push-ups, 10 sit-ups, dislocates. 5 rounds: 8 bench press, 8 pull-ups. Then with a partner for 16 minutes: 3 front squats, 3 burpees - continue by adding 3 repetitions of each movement until 16 minutes is up. Finish with a 9 minute row in groups of 3.

Home Edition:

- 2 rounds: 5 lunges each side, 10 push-ups, 10 sit-ups
- 5 rounds: 10 pike push-ups, 10 tricep dips
- Against a 16 minute clock (increasing 3 repetitions each round) 3 burpees, 3 floor switch kicks, 3 in and out abs
- Finish with max plank hold (try for at least 3 minutes)

DAY 153

Original Session: Warm up - 3 minute assault bike, then 2 rounds: 5 repetitions each: deadlift, row, power clean, front squat, push press. Work to a heavy power clean. Then at the top of every minute for 8 minutes: 3 power cleans at 60% of maximum effort. Next, perform burpee pull-ups - at the top of each minute, increase repetitions by 1. Go until failure to complete designated number in a minute

Home Edition:

- 40-30-20-10 repetitions of: burpees, air squats, push-ups, sit-ups
- Abdominal circuit: 1 minute each of: plank, straight leg sit-ups, ski abs, mountain climbers, russian twists, double leg lifts, standing oblique crunch (one minute each side)

DAY 154

Original Session: Warm up - 2 rounds: 30 second assault bike, 10 front squats, 10 push-ups, 5 kettlebell swings, 7 deadlifts, kettlebell farmer carries, sumo stretch, dislocates. Work to a heavy front squat, then 3 rounds: 1 front squat at 95% of maximum effort. Then, as many rounds as possible in 10 minutes: 3 ground to overheads, 3 pull-ups (increase each round by 3 repetitions of each).

Home Edition:

- 2 rounds: 30 second jog in place, 10 alternating lunges, 10 tricep dips, 10 glute bridge pulses
- Against a 20 minute clock, as many rounds as possible of: 3 jump squats, 3 pike push-ups, 3 butterfly sit-ups. Increase by 3 repetitions each round.

DAY 155

Original Session: Warm up - 5 minute 30 seconds on / 30 seconds off assault bike. 2 rounds: 10 thrusters, 10 pull-ups, 10 kettlebell swings, dislocates, instep stretch. Then, 5 rounds of: 12 thrusters, up in weight, 30 calorie row. Finish with 2 rounds: 8 pull-ups, 8 tricep dips, 8 dumbbell curl to press, 8 dumbbell flys.

Home Edition:

- 5 minute jog around your block or accumulate 5 minutes of jumping jacks, jog in place, high knees, butt kickers
- 5 rounds: 12 straight arm above head air squats, 1 minute sprint in place
- 2-4 rounds of: 8 push-ups, 8 floor switch kicks, 8 burpees, 8 plank shoulder taps

DAY 156

Original Session: Warm up - 3 minute assault bike, kettlebell swing ladder (10 swings each weight: 12k, 16k, 20k, 24k, 28k, 32k). Work to heavy deadlift. Then, 4 rounds of: 7 deadlifts at 70% of maximum effort, 50 double unders (150 singles). Finish with 50 weighted sit-ups.

Home Edition:

- 3 minute jog in place
- 4 rounds: 7 push-ups, 50 jumping jacks
- 100 sit-ups for time (shoot for 200 if feeling up for it)

DAY 157

Original Session: Warm up - 2 minute assault bike, 2 rounds of: 10 air squats, 10 push-ups, 10 box step ups, sumo stretch, 15 deadlifts. As many rounds as possible in 4 minutes of: 1) 10 box jumps, 10 kettlebell swings 2) 5 burpees, 5 power cleans 3) 30 double unders (90 singles) 4) 400 meter run, AMRAP goblet squats. Rest 4 minutes in between each set.

Home Edition:

- 2 rounds: 10 air squats, 10 push-ups, 10 glute bridge walk-outs
- As many rounds as possible in 4 minutes of: 10 jump squats, 10 pike push-ups
- As many rounds as possible in 4 minutes of: 5 burpees, 5 stance jacks
- As many rounds as possible in 4 minutes of: 30 jumping jacks, 10 frog jumps

DAY 158

Original Session: Warm up - 2 rounds: 250 meter row, 5 front squats, 5 push presses, 5 box jumps, sumo stretch, instep stretch. Work to a heavy front squat. Then, 3 rounds for time: 10 toes to bar, 10 front squats from ground, 10 burpees. Finish with 5 rounds of down and back prowler sprints.

Home Edition:

- 2 rounds: 3 minute jog, 5 air squats, 5 push-ups, 5 lunges each side
- 3 rounds: 10 double leg raises, 10 sit-ups, 10 burpees
- 5 rounds: 50 jumping jacks

DAY 159

Original Session: Warm up - At the top of each minute for 5 minutes: 5 push-ups, 5 air squats, gym down and back sprints, dislocates. Then, 5 rounds of: 5-10 pull-ups, 10 barbell row. 4 rounds: 12 deadlifts, 9 hang power cleans, 6 push jerks. Finish with 3 rounds of 10-15 Romanian deadlifts.

Home Edition:

- 100 burpees for time
- 15 minute abdominal circuit, your choice of 1 minute each: sit-ups, plank, side plank, straight leg sit-ups, v-ups, Russian twists, single leg raises, bicycle crunches, superman holds, hollow holds, flutter kicks, scissor kicks, janda sit-ups, scissor claps, switch kicks, ski abs, side plank pulses, standing oblique crunches, butterfly sit-ups, mountain climbers

DAY 160

Original Session: Warm up - At the top of each minute for 5 minutes: 5 push-ups, 5 air squats, down and back gym sprint. Then, with a partner alternate between the following until complete: 25 calorie assault bike while other partner completes as many back squats as possible, 25 calorie assault bike while other partner completes as many hang squat cleans as possible, 25 calorie assault bike while other partner completes as many deadlifts as possible, 25 calorie assault bike while other partner completes as many box jumps as possible, 25 calorie assault bike while other partner completes as many burpees as possible, 25 calorie assault bike while other partner completes as many weighted sit-ups as possible.

Home Edition:

- 25 jumping jacks, 25 air squats
- 25 jumping jacks, 25 burpees
- 25 squat jumps, 25 push-ups
- 25 squat jumps, 25 straight leg sit-ups

DAY 161

Original Session: Warm up - 5 minute assault bike, then 2 rounds of: 5 front squats, 5 strict press, 5 box jumps, instep stretch. Work to a heavy power clean, front squat, and jerk. Then, 3 rounds at 80% of maximum effort of power clean, front squat, and jerk. Finish with Fran: 21-15-9 thrusters and pull-ups.

Home Edition:

- 5 minute jog around your block, or accumulate 5 minutes of jumping jacks, mountain climbers, high knees, heisman
- 2 rounds: 5 air squats, 5 push-ups, 5 lunges each side
- 21-15-9 straight arms above head squats, pike push-ups or handstand push-ups if able

DAY 162

Original Session: Warm up - 500 meter row, then 2 rounds: 5 box jumps, 10 push-ups, 15 air squats, pigeon stretch. Then, 6 rounds of: 8 back squat, up in weight each round, 1 minute jump rope, 1 minute rest. For time: 30 box jumps, 30 kettlebell swings, 30 calorie assault bike

Home Edition:

- 5 minute jog
- 2 rounds: 5 jumping lunges each side, 15 air squats
- 6 rounds: 8 convict squats, 1 minute jumping jacks
- 30 push-ups, 60 mountain climbers, 90 high knees (may substitute for 75 burpees)

DAY 163

ALWAYS REMEMBER THIS…THERE IS ONLY ONE RECIPE FOR STRENGTH. A SECRET RECIPE THAT WAS HANDED DOWN FROM SANDOW TO JOHN GRIMEK TO PAUL ANDERSON TO VASILY ALEXEEV TO BILL KAZMAIER TO ME. NOW I'M GIVING YOU THAT MAGICAL RECIPE: HARD WORK PLUS PROPER NUTRITION PLUS TIME EQUALS STRONG. — STEVE PULCINELLA

Original Session: Warm up - 4 pull-ups, 6 push-ups, 8 lunges each side. With a partner, complete 100 calories on an assault bike. Then, 100 kettlebell swings each, 50 burpees combined, 100 box jumps combined, 50 deadlifts combined, 100 wall balls combined, 50 pull-ups combined (one works at a time). 100 walking lunges while resting or at the end, or any combination to get done.

Home Edition:

- 100 jumping jacks
- 50 air squats
- 50 burpees
- 50 side lunges each side
- 50 push-ups
- 100 sit-ups

DAY 164

Original Session: Warm up - 5 minute assault bike, then 2 rounds: 5 box step ups, 5 box jumps, 5 air squats, sumo stretch. Then, 8 rounds (30 seconds on, 10 seconds off) tabata row. Next, 3 rounds: 1 minute each station: box jumps, push presses, row, wall ball, tire smash or rope climb. 1 minute rest between rounds. Finish with 3 rounds - 25 weighted sit-ups, 25 butterfly sit-ups, 60 seconds plank, 30 seconds side plank each side.

Home Edition:

- 8 rounds: 30 seconds jumping jacks, 10 seconds rest
- 1 minute each: jump squats, push-ups, wall sits, glute bridge walk outs, walking push-ups
- 3 rounds - 25 straight arm sit-ups, 25 butterfly sit-ups, 60 seconds plank, 30 seconds side plank each side.

DAY 165

Original Session: Warm up - 2 minute assault bike, then two rounds of 10 lunges each side, 5 box jumps, 10 push-ups, 5 back squats. Work to a heavy single back squat. Then, complete 5 rounds of: 2 back squats at 70% of maximum effort, heavy sled push, rest 1 minute. Next, 2-4-6-8-10 repetitions of the following complex: deadlift, squat clean, push press, push-up. In between rounds, complete: 4-8-12-16-20 repetitions of pull-ups.

Home Edition:

- 2 rounds: 1 minute jog in place, 10 lunges each side, 5 air squats, 10 push-ups
- Accumulate 10 minutes in wall sits
- 2-4-6-8-10 repetitions of jump squats, jumping lunges, burpees. In between those rounds, complete: 4-6-8-12-16-20 repetitions of shoulder tap plank holds.

DAY 166

Original Session: Warm up - 2 rounds: 1 minute assault bike, 5/5 walking lunges, 5 deadlifts, sumo stretch, dislocates. Work to 70-80% of maximum deadlift. 6 rounds: 8 deadlifts, 2 minute row. Rest for 2 minutes between rounds. 5 rounds of down and back heavy sled push.

Home Edition:

- 2 rounds: 1 minute jumping jacks, 5/5 walking lunges, 5 arms overhead squats.
- 5 rounds: 20 burpees, 1 minute jog in place, 2 minute rest
- 100 sit-ups

DAY 167

Original Session: Warm up - 3 minute assault bike, then 2 rounds: 5 deadlifts, 5 hang cleans, 5 front squats, pigeon stretch. 5 rounds: 3 power cleans, up in weight each round. Finish with 3 rounds for time: 500 meter row, 15 box jumps, 12 burpees.

Home Edition:

- 3 minute jog around your block or accumulate 5 minutes of: jog in place, high knees, butt kickers
- 5 rounds: 3 wall walks (may substitute for 12 pike push-ups)
- 3 rounds: 75 jumping jacks, 15 tuck jumps, 12 burpees

DAY 168

> *SOME PEOPLE WANT IT TO HAPPEN, SOME WISH IT WOULD HAPPEN, OTHERS MAKE IT HAPPEN. — MICHAEL JORDAN*

Original Session: Warm up - 2 rounds: 30 second jump rope, 30 second assault bike, 10 air squats, 10 push-ups, instep stretch, dislocates. Work to a heavy thruster. Then, complete 4 rounds of 3 thrusters. For time: 2 rounds of: 42 wall balls, 24 pull-ups.

Home Edition:

- 2 rounds: 1 minute jumping jacks, 1 minute high knees, 10 air squats, 10 push-ups
- 50 unweighted squat thrusts
- 2 rounds: 42 burpees, 24 walking planks (12 each direction)

DAY 169

Original Session: Warm up - 10 goblet squats, 5/5 halo 10 lunges each side, 5/5 halo, 3 deadlifts. 80 heavy kettlebell swings (70#). 20 one-handed kettlebell swings, 10 Turkish get-ups.

Home Edition:

- 2 mile run or accumulate 15 minutes body weight movements of your choice (burpees, high knees, jumping jacks, butt kickers, heisman, jog in place)
- 50-40-30-20-10 repetitions of: air squats, push-ups, sit-ups

DAY 170

Original Session: Warm up - 3 rounds: 10 kettlebell swings, 10 lunges, 10 push-ups, 5 box jumps, instep stretch. With a partner, as many rounds as possible in 20 minutes of: 7 deadlifts, 5 hang squat cleans, 3 push presses. While partner 1 is working with the barbell, partner 2 assault bike sprints.

Home Edition:

- 3 rounds: 10 air squats, 10 lunges each side, 10 push-ups, 5 tuck jumps.
- Against a 20 minute clock, as many rounds as possible of the following: 7 burpees, 5 pike push-ups, 3 v-up sit-ups

DAY 171

Original Session: Warm up - 3 rounds: 5 box jumps, 10 push-ups, 5 pull-ups, 10 air squats. As many rounds as possible in 9 minutes of: 5 pull-ups, 10 burpee box jumps, 15 goblet squats. As many rounds as possible in 6 minutes of: 7 pull-ups, 12 burpee box jumps, 17 goblet squats. As many rounds as possible in 3 minutes of: 9 pull-ups, 14 burpee box jumps, 19 goblet squats. 2 rounds: 250 meter maximum ski er

Home Edition:

- 3 rounds: 5 jump squats, 10 push-ups, 5 burpees, 10 air squats
- As many rounds as possible in 9 minutes of: 5 push-ups, 10 burpees, 15 air squats
- As many rounds as possible in 6 minutes of: 7 push-ups, 12 burpees, 17 air squats
- As many rounds as possible in 3 minutes of: 9 push-ups, 14 burpees, 19 air squats

DAY 172

> *BEING NEGATIVE AND LAZY IS A DISEASE THAT LEADS TO PAIN, HARDSHIPS, DEPRESSION, POOR HEALTH AND FAILURE. BE PROACTIVE AND GIVE A DAMN TO ACHIEVE SUCCESS! — PHIL HEATH*

Original Session: Warm up - 2 minute assault bike, then 2 rounds of: 5 hang squat cleans, 5 push presses, 5 box jumps, 5/5 lunges. Work to a heavy squat clean & jerk. Then, 5 rounds of: 1 squat clean & jerk. Pick your poison: 150 wall balls, 30 ground to overhead, or 50 thrusters and 30 pull-ups. Finish with a 1,000 meter row.

Home Edition:

- 2 minute jumping jacks, then 2 rounds: 5 air squats, 5 push-ups, 5 jump squats
- Your choice of: 150 burpees, 300 air squats, or 100 push-ups

DAY 173

Original Session: Warm up - 2 rounds: 5 push presses, 5 bent over rows, 5/5 lunges, 5 push-ups, dislocates. 5-5-3-3-1-1-1 strict presses, increasing weight each set. 5/5 kettlebell rows in between each set. 50 kettlebell swings, 10 toes to bar, 20 double unders. 40 kettlebell swings, 10 toes to bar, 20 double unders. 30 kettlebell swings, 10 toes to bar, 20 double unders. 200 kettlebell swings, 10 toes to bar, 20 double unders. 10 kettlebell swings, 10 toes to bar, 20 double unders. Finish with (to failure) plank holds - 45 seconds on, 20 seconds off.

Home Edition:

- 2 rounds: 5 push-ups, 5/5 lunges, 10 air squats
- 50-40-30-20-10 repetitions of: burpees, sit ups
- Finish with plank holds 45 second on, 20 seconds rest until failure

DAY 174

Original Session: Warm up - 5 minute assault bike. 6 rounds: 8 deadlifts (up in weight) 2 minute assault bike, 2 minute rest. 4 rounds: heavy prowler relay.

Home Edition:

- 5 minute jog around your block, or accumulate 5 minutes jogging in place, jumping jacks, high knees
- 6 rounds: 18 tuck jumps, 2 minute jumping jacks, 1 minute plank hold
- Max handstand hold (try for as many rounds as possible of 30 seconds - 1 minute)

DAY 175

Original Session: Warm up - 2 rounds: 5 power cleans, 10 push-ups, 5 box jumps, 10/10 lunges, instep stretch. Work to a working weight front squat, then 5 rounds of 3 front squats, up in weight. 4 rounds: as many rounds as possible in 3 minute sof: 3 power cleans, 6 box jumps, 9 pull-ups or ring rows.

Home Edition:

- 2 rounds: 5 air squats, 5 push-ups, 10 sit-ups
- 5 rounds: 5 slow push-ups with a hand release at the bottom
- 4 rounds, 3 minutes each. Complete as many rounds as possible of: 3 burpees, 6 jump squats, 9 sit-ups

DAY 176

Original Session: Warm up - 3 minute assault bike, then 2 rounds of: 5 ring rows, 5 push-ups, 5/5 lunges, dislocates, instep stretch. Then, 5 rounds of: 5 weighted pull-ups, 5 weighted tricep dips. With a partner, row 5,000 meters.

Home Edition:

- 3 minute jog around your block or accumulate 5 minutes of jogging in place
- 5 rounds: 5 push-ups, 10 tricep dips
- 2 mile run or 150 burpees

DAY 177

Original Session: Warm up - 2 rounds: 30 second assault bike, 5/5 box step ups, 5 front squats, sumo stretch. 5 rounds: 6 front squats, up in weight, 30 second assault bike sprint, 2 minute rest. For time: 30 burpees, 40 wall balls, 50 kettlebell swings.

Home Edition:

- 4 minute jog around your block, or accumulate 5 minutes of jumping jacks, high knees, jog in place, heisman, butt kickers
- 5 rounds: 10 slow air squats
- 30 burpees, 60 lunges, (30 each side) 120 sit-ups

DAY 178

Original Session: Warm up - At the top of each minute for 5 minutes: 5 push-ups, 5 air squats, 1 gym length sprint. With a partner: 1,000 meter combined row, 30 burpees, 40 box jumps, 50 back squat. 1,000 combined meter row, 30/30 lunges, 40 toes to bar, 50 deadlifts. 1,000 combined meter row. Every movement each partner completes all repetitions with the exception of combined row.

Home Edition:

- Every minute for 5 minutes, complete 5 push-ups, 5 air squats, 3/3 lunges
- 50 jumping jacks, 30 burpees, 40 air squats, 50 sit-ups
- 50 jumping jacks, 30 walking push-ups, 40 double leg lifts, 50 sit-ups
- 50 jumping jacks

DAY 179

Original Session: Warm up - 2 rounds: 1 minute assaul bike, 5 pull-ups, 10 lunges, 10 kettlebell swings, 5 push-ups. 5 rounds, as many rounds as possible in 3 minutes of: 250 meter row, 3 power cleans, 6 push-ups, 9 air squats. Finish with one minute all out assault bike sprint.

Home Edition:

- 2 rounds: 5 pike push-ups, 5/5 lunges, 10 air squats
- 5 rounds: As many rounds as possible in 3 minutes: 30 second sprint in place, 3 tuck jumps, 6 push-ups, 9 air squats
- 2 minute all out sprint in place or as many burpees possible in 3 minutes

DAY 180

Original Session: Warm up - 5 minutes 30 seconds on/30 seconds off assault bike, then 2 rounds: 5 pull-ups, 10 push-ups, 15 air squats. Work to a heavy back squat. Then, 5 rounds of 3 back squats, 1 heavy prowler sprint. Next, 10-9-8-7-6-5-4-3-2-1 repetitions of: thrusters, toes to bar.

Home Edition:

- 5 minute light jog around your block or accumulate 5 minutes jog in place
- 2 rounds: 5 push-ups, 10 sit-ups, 15 air squats
- 10-9-8-7-6-5-4-3-2-1 repetitions of: arm raise air squats, double leg raises, glute bridge walk outs

DAY 181

Original Session: Warm up - 2 rounds: 5 box jumps, 5 hang squat cleans, 10 lunges, 5 pull-ups, sumo stretch, dislocates. 3 rounds: 5 hang squat cleans, 3 max box jumps, 2 minute row, rest 2 minutes. 3 rounds: 8 body weight deadlifts, 10 push-ups, 90 second gym length sprints, rest 1 minute. 3 rounds: 10 burpees, 10 dumbbell thruster, 10 pull-ups

Home Edition:

- 2 rounds: 5 jump squats, 5 air squats, 5/5 lunges, 5 push-ups
- 3 rounds: 5 tuck jumps, 3/3 jumping lunges, 2 minutes jumping jacks
- 3 rounds: 8 pike push-ups, 10 tricep dips, 90 second sprint in place
- 3 rounds: 10 burpees, 10 unweighted thrusters, 10 walking plank

DAY 182

YOU HAVE TO PUSH PAST YOUR PERCEIVED LIMITS, PUSH PAST THAT POINT YOU THOUGHT WAS AS FAR AS YOU CAN GO. — DREW BREES

Original Session: Warm up - At the top of each minute for 5 minutes: 5 push-ups, 5 air squats, 5 box jumps. 500 meter row, then: 5 rounds: 10 ground to overhead, 20 air squats, 10 pull-ups. Finish with a 500 meter row. Finish with 50 calories for time on the assault bike.

Home Edition:

- At the top of each minute for 5 minutes: 5 push-ups, 5 air squats, 5 box jumps.
- 3 minute jog in place
- 5 rounds: 10 right/10 left arms overhead walking lunges, 20 air squats, 10 push-ups
- 3 minute jumping jacks

DAY 183

Original Session: Warm up - 5 box jumps, 10 kettlebell swings, 10 air squats, 10 push presses. With a partner: Partner 1 rows 250 meter while partner works on the following: 150 wall balls, 21-15-9 thrusters and pull-ups, 30 ground to overheads. Partners switch evey 250 meters until repetitions of all movements are complete.

Home Edition:

- 5 jump squats, 10 push-ups, 20 air squats
- 4 minute jog around your block, or 40 burpees
- 150 air squats
- 21-15-9 repetitions of: tricep dips, sit-ups
- 30 tuck jumps

DAY 184

Original Session: Warm up - 5 minute assault bike, then 2 rounds: 5 hang squat cleans, 5 box jumps, 10 lunges. Practice squat clean progression technique. Then, at the top of every minute for 5 minutes, perform 2 squat cleans at 70-80% of maximum effort. Next, in 4 minutes, complete a maximum number of burpee box jumps, rest 3 minutes. In 3 minutes, complete a maximum number of wall balls, rest 2 minutes. In 2 minutes, complete maximum gym length sprints, rest 1 minute. Finish with maximum number of pull-ups in 1 minute.

Home Edition:

- 5 minute jog around your block or 5 minutes jog in place, high knees, jumping jacks, butt kickers, heisman
- Against a 4 minute clock, maximum burpees. Against a 3 minute clock, air squats. Against a 2 minute clock, maximum jumping jacks. Against a 1 minute clock, perform maximum sit-ups.

DAY 185

Original Session: Warm up - 2 rounds: 1 minute assault bike. 5 push presses, 5 push-ups, dislocates, sumo stretch. 5 rounds: push press up in weight each round, pull-ups/ring rows. Finish with 3 rounds of: 21-15-9 repetitions of: assault bike calories, wall balls, box jumps.

Home Edition:

- 2 rounds: 1 minute each of: jog in place, push-ups, sit-ups
- 21-15-9 repetitions of: air squats, push-ups
- 3 rounds: 1 minute sit-ups, 1 minute plank, 1 minute ski abs

DAY 186

Original Session: Warm up - 30 seconds jump rope, 10 lunges, 5 push-ups, sumo, instep. Then, complete 4 rounds of: 8 lunges each side with double front rack kettlebells followed by one heavy forward and backward heavy sled pull, 90 second rest. Next, 4 rounds of: 10 kettlebell chest presses, one rope climb, 2 minute sandbag get up, 90 second rest. Finish with 5 rounds: 5 burpees, 5 gym length sprints.

Home Edition:

- 30 seconds jumping jacks, 5 lunges each side, 5 push-ups
- 4 rounds: 8 lunges each side, 8 push-ups
- 4 rounds: 1 minute wall sit hold
- 5 rounds: 5 burpees, 1 minute sprint in place

DAY 187

Original Session: Warm up - 15 seconds each: lunges, push-ups, air squats, rest. Then work to a one rep max in the following complex: high hang clean, hang clean, squat clean from the ground. At the top of each minute for 20 minutes: odd numbers = 16 calorie assault bike, even numbers = 5 squat cleans at 70% of maximum effort. Finish with 3 rounds of: 20 GHD sit-ups or weighted sit-ups, 30 second L-sit, 30 second plank.

Home Edition:

- 15 seconds each: lunges, push-ups, air squats
- At the top of each minute for 20 minutes: Odd numbers = sprint in place, even numbers = burpees.
- 3 rounds: 20 sit-ups, 20 tricep dips, 1 minute plank

DAY 188

Original Session: Warm up - 500 meter row, then 2 rounds: 5 deadlifts, 10 air squats, 5 pull-ups, 5 push-ups, instep stretch. Work to a heavy set of 3 deadlifts. Then complete 6-9-12-15 repetitions of heavy deadlifts and double unders. Finish with 50 toes to bar.

Home Edition:

- 4 minute jog around your block, or complete 150 jumping jacks
- 2 rounds: 10 air squats, 5 pike push-ups, 5 sit-ups
- 6-9-12-15 repetitions of: handstand wall walks, pulse squats
- 50 burpees

DAY 189

Original Session: Warm up - 500 meter row, then 2 rounds: 10 goblet squat, 10 kettlebell swing, 10 push-ups, instep stretch. With a partner, complete: 1,000 meter row, 50 pull-ups, 100 ball slams, 50 push-ups, 100 kettlebell swings, 50 box jumps, 1,000 m row.

Home Edition:

- 5 minute jog around your block, or accumulate 5 minutes of jog in place, high knees, jumping jacks, butt kickers, heisman
- 100 jumping jacks, 25 burpees, 100 air squats, 25 push-ups, 25 lunges each side, 25 tricep dips, 100 jumping jacks

DAY 190

Original Session: Warm up - At the top of each minute for 5 minutes: 3 burpees, 1 gym length sprint. Then, complete 5 rounds of: 5 pull-ups, 10 push-ups (alternate between diamond, spider, hand release). Then, complete a fight gone bad: 3 rounds, 1 minute at each station: kettlebell swings, box jumps, weighted sit-ups, double unders, wall balls. Then, 3 rounds: 10 hanging leg raises, 30 second plank, 30 seconds side plank each side.

Home Edition:

- At the top of each minute for 5 minutes, complete 3 burpees, 3 sit-ups
- 5 rounds: 10 push-up (alternate between the following variations: standard, hand release, diamond, side to side, arm raise plank push-ups)
- 3 rounds, 1 minute each movement: stance jacks, jumping lunges, floor switch kicks, glute bridge walk outs
- 3 rounds: 10 leg raises, 30 second front plank, 30 seconds side plank each side

DAY 191

Original Session: Warm up - 500 meter row, then 2 rounds of: 5 power cleans, 5 push presses, 5 box jumps. 3 rounds: 6 power cleans, up in weight, 12 push-ups, 2 minute assault bike, 2 minute rest. Then, 3 rounds: 8 deadlift, up in weight, 3 minute row, 2 minute rest. Finish with 3 rounds: 20 wall balls, 10 box jumps.

Home Edition:

- 1 minute each: jog in place, jump squats, push-ups
- 3 rounds: 6 burpees, 12 switch kicks, two minute sprint in place
- 3 rounds: 8 leg lifts, 3 minute jumping jacks
- 3 rounds: 20 air squats, 10 sit-ups

DAY 192

Original Session: Warm up - 30 seconds fast/30 seconds slow assault bike for 5 minutes, foam roll, dislocates. 5 rounds of 3-7 push press up in weight, 5 pull-ups. Then, at the top of each minute for 10 minutes, 5 handstand push-ups, 15 heavy kettlebell swings, 20 air squats. Finish with 4 rounds of: 250 meter max row.

Home Edition:

- 4 minute jog around your block or 4 minutes jog in place
- At the top of each minute for 10 minutes: 5 pike push-ups, 15 sit-ups, 20 air squats
- 4 rounds: Max burpees in one minute

DAY 193

Original Session: Warm up - 2 rounds: 1 minute assault bike, 5 squat cleans, 10 lunges, 5 box jumps, pigeon stretch. Work to a heavy clean and jerk. Then 7 rounds: squat clean, front squat, jerk. Finish with a 20 minute heavy prowler relay.

Home Edition:

- 2 rounds: 20 stance jacks, 10 air squats, 5 push-ups
- Accumulate 3-5 minutes in wall handstand hold or perform as many push-ups in 5 minutes as possible
- 100 sit-ups for time

DAY 194

Original Session: Warm up - 500 meter row, then 3 rounds: 10 kettlebell swings, 15 mountain climbers, 10 overhead plate lunges. Next, complete 5 rounds of 5 overhead squats. Finish with 7 rounds of: 7 burpees, 9 wall balls, 11 plate Russian twists, 13 double unders.

Home Edition:

- 5 minute jog around your block or 5 minute jog in place, 10 lunges, 10 mountain climbers, ten convict squats
- 7 rounds: 7 burpees, 9 air squats 11 russian twists, 13 leg raises

DAY 195

Original Session: Warm up - 10 minute assault bike, 5 push-ups, 5 box jumps. With a partner, complete: 100 kettlebell swings, 80 calorie row, 60 deadlifts, 40 burpees, 80 pull-ups, 100 wall balls.

Home Edition:

- 2 mile run for time (may substitute 300 burpees)

DAY 196

Original Session: Warm up - Thunderstruck burpees. For the duration of the song, perform a burpee every time the word *Thunderstruck* is said. 5 rounds: 10 pull-ups, 20 push-ups, 30 sit-ups, 40 air squats, 2 minute rest. 5 rounds: gymnastic complex: pushup, wall walk, shoulder taps, reverse wall walk.

Home Edition:

- Pick any song with a repetitive word such as *Thunderstruck* and perform your movement of choice each time that word is said (air squats, burpees, push-ups, sit-ups..etc)
- 5 rounds: 10 tricep dips, 20 push-ups, 30 sit-ups, 40 air squats
- 5 rounds gymnastic complex: pushup, wall walk, shoulder taps, reverse wall walk

DAY 197

Original Session: Warm up - 3 minute assault bike, then 2 rounds: 5 push-ups, 10 air squat, 10 sit-ups, pigeon stretch, instep stretch. Work to a heavy front squat. Then, 2-4-6-8-10 repetitions of: front squat, followed by alternating: 20-16-12-8 burpee box jumps. Finish with 3 rounds of maximum L-sit for time.

Home Edition:

- 3 minute jumping jacks, then 2 rounds of: 5 push-ups, 10 air squats, 10 sit-ups
- 2-4-6-8-10 repetitions of: jump squats
- 20-16-12-8 burpees
- 3 rounds: maximum handstand hold or wall sit

DAY 198

THE OBSTACLE IN THE PATH BECOMES THE PATH. NEVER FORGET, WITHIN EVERY OBSTACLE IS AN OPPORTUNITY TO IMPROVE OUR CONDITION. — RYAN HOLIDAY

Original Session: Warm up - 2 rounds: 250 meter row, 10 push-ups, 10 air squats, 5 box jumps. Then, work to a heavy set of 5 bench presses. Next, 5 rounds: 5 bench presses at 90% of maximum effort, 10 kettlebell rows. Complete 1,000 meter row, 2 rounds of: 40 wall balls, 60 double unders, finish with 1,000 meter row. Finally, end with 2 rounds of 10 each side glute raises

Home Edition:

- 1 minute jog in place, 10 push-ups, 10 air squats, 5 jump squats, 1 minute jog in place
- 5 rounds: 5 hand release push-ups
- 1 minute each: stance jacks, high knees, butt kickers, frog hops
- 2 rounds: 40 air squats, 60 jumping jacks
- 1 minute each: stance jacks, high knees, butt kickers, frog hops

DAY 199

Original Session: Warm up - 2 rounds: 1 minute assault bike, 5 burpees, 5 box jumps, instep stretch. 6 rounds: 6 deadlift up in weight, 3 box jumps up in height. At the top of each minute for 20 minutes: 30 seconds wall balls or kettlebell swings, 30 seconds rest, 30 seconds dumbbell man makers, 30 seconds rest. Finish with 3 rounds: 30 second max assault bike.

Home Edition:

- 2 rounds: 5 burpees, 5 push-ups, 10 sit-ups
- At the top of each minute for 20 minutes: 30 air squats, 30 seconds rest, 30 sit-ups, 30 seconds rest
- Finish with 3 minutes sprint in place or sprint around your block

DAY 200

Original Session: Warm up - 3 rounds: 5 burpees, 5 box jumps, 10 push-ups, 10 lunges each side. Then complete: 20 box jumps, 2 burpees, 18 box jumps, 4 burpees, 16 box jumps, 6 burpees, 14 box jumps, 8 burpees . . . continue until 2 box jumps and 20 burpees are complete. Finish with 3 rounds of: 3 turkish get ups each side, 10 good mornings, 15 alternating arch ups.

Home Edition:

- 20 air squats, 2 burpees, 18 air squats, 4 burpees, 16 air squats, 6 burpees, 14 air squats, 8 burpees . . Continue until 2 box jumps and 20 burpees are complete.
- 3 rounds:1 minute hollow hold, 1 minute superman hold, 30 seconds each side one leg glute bridge hold

DAY 201

Original Session: Warm up - 5 minutes: 30 seconds fast, 30 seconds moderate assault bike. Then, complete 3 rounds of: 8 front squat up in weight, 4 box jumps, 2 minute row, 2 minute rest. Next, 3 rounds: 8 deadlift up in weight, 2 minute weighted step ups, 2 minute rest. Finish with as many rounds possible in 6 minutes of: 20 overhead kettlebell swings, 5 gym length sprints

Home Edition:

- 3 rounds: 20 air squats, 5 jump squats
- 3 rounds: 20 moving push-ups, 5 burpees
- 100 sit-ups

DAY 202

THE PATH TO SUCCESS IS TO TAKE MASSIVE, DETERMINED ACTIONS. — TONY ROBBINS

Original Session: Warm up - At the top of each minute for 5 minutes: 5 push-ups, 5 air squats, 5 box jumps. Then, 6 rounds: 3 push presses up in weight, 1 rope climb. 2 rounds: 50 air squats, 40 calorie row, 30 box jumps, 20 burpees, 10 toes to bar

Home Edition:

- At the top of each minute for 5 minutes: 5 push-ups, 5 air squats, 20 second sprint
- 3 rounds: 50 air squats, 40 sit-ups, 30 total lunges, 10 leg raises

DAY 203

Original Session: Warm up - At the top of each minute for 5 minutes, perform 5 push-ups, 5 air squats, 5 box jumps. Then, work to a heavy hang squat clean. Next, 5 rounds of 1 hang squat clean, up in weight each round. Followed by 5 rounds of: 12 wall balls, 12 burpees. Finish with 3 rounds of 20 Russian twists with plate.

Home Edition:

- At the top of each minute for 5 minutes: 5 push-ups, 5 air squats, 5 sit-ups
- 5 rounds: 30 second wall sit hold
- 5 rounds: 12 floor switch kicks, 12 burpees
- 1 minute each: v-up-sit-ups, front plank, unweighted Russian twists, standing oblique crunch, ski abs, side plank left, side plank right

DAY 204

> *SELF-DISCIPLINE IS AN ACT OF CULTIVATION. IT REQUIRES YOU TO CONNECT TODAY'S ACTIONS TO TOMORROW'S RESULTS. THERE'S A SEASON FOR SOWING, A SEASON FOR REAPING. SELF-DISCIPLINE HELPS YOU KNOW WHICH IS WHICH. — GARY RYAN BLAIR*

Original Session: Warm up - 5 minute assault bike. Snatch Density work: 15:15 MVO2 Protocol. @18# 80 rounds - 15 seconds snatch - (9x), 15 seconds rest - 720 snatches total.

Home Edition:

- 300 burpees for time

DAY 205

Original Session: Warm up - 2 rounds: 4 gym length sprints, 10 mountain climbers, 10 air squats, 10 up down planks. 3 rounds: 250 meter row, 10 wall balls, 5 inverted push-ups, 10 goblet lunges. 3 rounds, 1 minute jump rope, 10 renegade rows, 10 ball slams, 1 rope climb. Finish with 5 rounds: 10 surrenders, 1 down and back kettlebell farmer carry.

Home Edition:

- 2 rounds: 1 minute jog in place, 10 mountain climbers, 10 air squats, 10 up and down planks
- 3 rounds: 4 minute jog around your block or 3 minute jog in place, 10 air squats, 5 pike push ups
- 3 rounds: 1 minute jumping jacks, 10 moving planks, 10 lunges each side
- 25 burpees

DAY 206

Original Session: Warm up - 3 minute assault bike, kettlebell swing ladder (5 swings up in weight each set, 4 gym shuttle sprints). Work to a heavy hang squat clean. Then, at the top of each minute for 10 minutes complete 3 hang squat cleans. 3 rounds: 1 minute max assault bike, 1 minute kettlebell goblet squats, one minute rest. 3 rounds: 1 minute max row, 1 minute kettlebell or dumbbell snatches, rest one minute

Home Edition:

- 5 minute jog around your block or jog in place, 10 air squats, 10 sit ups, 5 push-ups
- 50-40-30-20-10 repetitions of: air squats, floor switch kicks, straight leg sit ups

DAY 207

Original Session: Warm up - 3 minute assault bike. 3 rounds: 10 air squats, 5 push-ups, pigeon stretch, dislocates. 3 rounds: 10 dumbbell thrusters, 1 minute row, 90 seconds rest. 3 rounds: 10 deadlifts up in weight, 1 minute shuttle sprints, 1 minute rest. 3 rounds: 10 tricep dips, 10 curl to press, 10 toes to bar, 10 GHD hip extensions

Home Edition:

- 3 minutes jumping jacks
- 3 rounds: 10 air squats, 5 push-ups, 5 sit ups
- 3 rounds: 10 pike push-ups, one minute sprint in place
- 3 rounds: 10 tricep dips, 1 minute plank hold, 10 leg raises, 20 butt kickers each side

DAY 208

Original Session: Warm up - 1 minute assault bike, 10 dislocates, 10 overhead squats, 10 sots press. 5 rounds: 6 overhead squat up in weight each round. Then, 21-15-9 repetitions of: Dumbbell thrusters, pull-ups. Finish with max plank hold.

Home Edition:

- 1 minute each: sprint in place, high knees, butt kickers, side to side lunges
- 5 rounds: 20 behind the head air squats
- 21-15-9 repetitions of: push-ups, bicycle crunches
- Max plank hold (try and shoot for 3-5 minutes)

DAY 209

Original Session: Warm up - 2 rounds: 30 second jump rope, 5 deadlifts, 5 walking lunges each side, instep stretch, pigeon stretch. 6 rounds: 4 back squats up in weight, 4 box jumps up in height. 100 calorie buy in, then as many rounds as possible in 14 minutes of: 5/5 kettlebell clean and press, 20 wall balls, 10 kettlebell weighted sit-ups.

Home Edition:

- 2 rounds: 30 seconds jumping jacks, 5 walking lunges each side, 5 sit-ups
- 6 rounds: 8 jump squats
- 8 minute jog around your block, then as many rounds as possible in 14 minutes of: 5 pike push-ups, 20 second wall sit holds, 10 sit-ups

DAY 210

Original Session: Warm up - 30 seconds assault bike, 5 lunges each side, 5 burpees, instep stretch. 4 rounds: 8 kettlebell floor press each side, 20 seconds assault bike. With a partner, 7 minutes each station: 2 for 1 wall ball, row, assault bike.

Home Edition:

- 30 seconds jog in place, 5 lunges each side, 5 push-ups
- For time: 200 burpees

DAY 211

Original Session: Warm up - 6 shuttle runs, 5 push-ups, 10 air squats, 5 lunges each side. Then, in teams of 3: 100 calorie assault bike, 100 ball slams, 200 air squats, 100 pull-ups. 15 minute alternating farmer carries

Home Edition:

- 5 minute jog around your block (or 1 minute each of: jog in place, high knees, butt kickers, heisman, frog jumps)
- 20 jumping lunges each side, 20 bicycle crunches, 20 push-ups
- 4 rounds: 30 seconds each: front plank, side plank left, side plank right

DAY 212

Original Session: Warm up - 2 rounds: 250 meter row, 5 front squats, 5 lunges each side, 5 jumping pull ups, dislocates, instep. Then, 5 rounds: 3 front squats, up in weight each round, 30 seconds sprint. Rest as needed. At the top of each minute for 10 minutes, 15 wall balls, 5-10 pull-ups. Finish with at the top of each minute for 10 minutes, 15 kettlebell swings, 10 box jumps.

Home Edition:

- 2 rounds: 1 minute each - jumping jacks, air squats, walking lunges, push-ups.
- 5 rounds: 10 air squats, sprint in place for 30 seconds
- At the top of each minute for 10 minutes: 15 mountain climbers, 10 tricep dips
- At the top of each minute for 10 minutes: 5 pike push-ups, 10 jumping lunges

DAY 213

> *TRUST YOURSELF. CREATE THE KIND OF SELF THAT YOU WILL BE HAPPY TO LIVE WITH ALL YOUR LIFE. MAKE THE MOST OF YOURSELF BY FANNING THE TINY, INNER SPARKS OF POSSIBILITY INTO FLAMES OF ACHIEVEMENT. — GOLDA MEIR*

Original Session: Warm up - 2 rounds: 250 meter row, 5 deadlifts, 5 box jumps, instep, dislocates. Then, complete as many pull-ups as possible in 15 minutes. Finish with 21-15-9 repetitions of: Deadlifts, box jumps, assault bike calories.

Home Edition:

- 2 minutes jog in place, 10 unweighted good mornings, 10 air squats.
- Complete as many push-ups as possible in 15 minutes
- 21-15-9 repetitions of: floor switch kicks, v-up sit-ups, glute bridge walk outs

DAY 214

Original Session: Warm up - At the top of every minute for 5 minutes: 5 push-ups, 5 air squats, 4 gym sprints. Then, 3 rounds: 8 back squats up in weight each round, 30 seconds moderate/30 seconds fast row, 90 seconds rest. Finish with 3 rounds of rope complex: 20 slams, 20/20 side to side, 20 jumping jacks.

Home Edition:

- At the top of each minute for 5 minutes: 5 push-ups, 5 air squats, 5 jumping jacks
- 3 rounds: 10 side lunges each side, 1 minute sprint in place
- 50 burpees for time

DAY 215

Original Session: Warm up - 5 pull-ups, 10 push-ups, 10 air squats, instep, dislocates. Then with a partner, complete 100 calorie row or assault bike. With remaining time, as many repetitions as possible in 5 minutes at the following stations: kettlebell swings, pull-ups, air squats, burpees.

Home Edition:

- 3 rounds: 10 push-ups, 10 air squats, 10 sit-ups
- Jog around your block for 10 minutes, or build 10 minutes of movements of your choice (butt kickers, heisman, mountain climbers, jumping jacks, high knees, jumping lunges, etc)
- Against a 5 minute clock for each movement, as many repetitions as you can get in: jumping lunges, straight leg sit-ups, burpees, standing oblique crunches

DAY 216

Original Session: Warm up - 500 meter row, lungess complex, dislocates, around the worlds, overhead squats. Then with a partner, complete 1/1, 2/2, 3/3…..etc of thrusters and burpees until failure. Then, 6 rounds: 5 squat cleans, 10 pull-ups, 250 meter row (switch partners each round). Finish with 30 second handstand holds, 45 seconds hollow holds, 45 seconds superman holds.

Home Edition:

- 3 minute jog around your block or 3 minutes jumping jacks
- 10 rounds: 2 unweighted thrusters, 4 burpees
- 6 rounds: 5 push-ups
- 3 rounds: 30 seconds hollow holds, 30 seconds superman holds

DAY 217

NOBLE AND GREAT. COURAGEOUS AND DETERMINED. FAITHFUL AND FEARLESS. THAT IS WHO YOU ARE AND WHO YOU HAVE ALWAYS BEEN. AND UNDERSTANDING IT CAN CHANGE YOUR LIFE BECAUSE THIS KNOWLEDGE CARRIES A CONFIDENCE THAT CANNOT BE DUPLICATED ANY OTHER WAY. — SHERI L. DEW

Original Session: Warm up - 30 seconds jump rope, 30 seconds assault bike, 5 lunges each side, sumo stretch, instep stretch. Then, 5 rounds: 3 squat cleans up in weight each round. Next, complete 4 rounds of: 400 meter run followed by 12 kettlebell swings, 12 box jumps against a 4 minute clock. Finish with 3 rounds of: 8 toes to bar, 60 seconds plank.

Home Edition:

- 30 seconds jump rope or jump in place, 30 seconds jog in place, 5 lunges each side.
- 4 rounds: 20 burpees, 20 tricep dips, 10 plank shoulder taps each side
- Abdominal circuit - 2 minutes each: single leg raises, double leg raises, bicycles, plank holds of choice, standing oblique crunches (one minute each side)

DAY 218

Original Session: Warm up - 3 rounds - 5 push presses, 5 push-ups, 5 ring rows, med ball shoulder stretch, instep. Work to a heavy push press. Then 4 rounds of: 4 push presses at 70% of maximum effort. Next, as many rounds as possible in 18 minutes of: 25 calorie assault bike, 7 burpees, 2 rope climbs (or 10 ring rows).

Home Edition:

- 3 rounds: 5 push-ups, 10 walking lunges, 30 second wall sit hold
- As many rounds as possible in 18 minutes of: 1 minute sprint in place, 7 burpees, 5 straight leg sit-ups.

DAY 219

Original Session: Warm up - 10 back squats, 10 kettlebell swings, child's pose, instep. Then, 5 rounds of: 5 back squats at 70% of maximum effort. Next, row complex: 4,500 meters total of: 500m sprint, 500m moderate, 250m sprint, 250m moderate (repeat for a total of 3 rounds).

Home Edition:

- 200 burpees for time

DAY 220

Original Session: Warm up - 400 meter run, then 2 rounds: 10 air squats, 5 jump squats, 10 push-ups, dislocates, banded walks. Then, 5 rounds of: 5 kettlebell strict press, 5 second negative pull down. Next, 5 rounds of: 5 kettlebell row, 5 second negative let down. Finish with as many rounds as possible with a partner in 18 minutes of: 400 meter sandbag run while the other partner completes as many rounds as possible of 5 deadlifts, 10 box jumps, 2 rope climbs.

Home Edition:

- 3 minute jog around your block or jog in place
- 2 rounds: 10 air squats, 5 jump squats, 10 push-ups
- 5 rounds: 5-10 slow push-ups, pausing at the bottom for 3-5 seconds before rising up
- 40-30-20-10 repetitions of: mountain climbers, side to side lunges, plank shoulder taps, double leg raises

DAY 221

> *THERE'S NOT A PERSON ON MY TEAM IN 16 YEARS THAT HAS CONSISTENTLY BEAT ME TO THE BALL EVERY PLAY. THAT AIN'T GOT NOTHING TO DO WITH TALENT, THAT'S JUST GOT EVERYTHING TO DO WITH EFFORT, AND NOTHING ELSE. — RAY LEWIS*

Original Session: Warm up - 2 rounds: 400 meter run, 10 air squats, 10 push-ups, 10 box jumps, dislocates, sumo stretch. 3 rounds: 60 seconds each: handstand holds, wall sit, plank. Then, 2 rounds: 20 overhead kettlebell swings, 20 goblet squat thrusters, 20 lunges each side, 10 one leg deadlift each side, 20 Russian twists each side, 20 sit-ups. Finish with 10 minute prowler relay.

Home Edition:

- 4 minute jog around your block or accumulate 4 minutes of: stance jacks, heisman, butt kickers, high knees
- 3 rounds, 60 seconds each: handstand holds, wall sit, plank
- 20 air squats, 20 hands overhead lunges each side, 10 unweighted one leg deadlifts each side, 20 unweighted Russian twists each side, 20 sit-ups.
- Max plank shoulder taps in 10 minutes

DAY 222

Original Session: Warm up - 2 rounds: 1 minute row, 8 push-ups, 8 sit-ups, 8 kettlebell swings, sumo stretch. Then, complete 6 rounds of: 8 deadlifts up in weight each round. Next, 4 rounds of: 10 push presses, 75 double unders (or 150 singles). Finish with 4 rounds of 20 second dragonfly holds.

Home Edition:

- 2 rounds: 1 minute jog in place, 8 push-ups, 8 sit-ups, 8 L-sit raises.
- 6 rounds: 30 second - 1 minute handstand holds
- 4 rounds: 10 diamond push-ups, 100 jumping jacks.
- 4 rounds: 30 second flutter kicks

DAY 223

Original Session: Warm up - 500 meter row, then 2 rounds: 5 ring rows, 5 lunges each side, dislocates, instep stretch. Then, 4 rounds of: 10 front rack kettlebell lunges right, 10 front rack kettlebell lunges left. 3 rounds: 25 calorie row, 25 wall balls, 6 gym length double kettlebell farmer carries. Finish with 3 rounds of 35 leg taps.

Home Edition:

- 5 minute jog around your block or run in place
- 2 rounds: 5 push-ups, 5 lunges each side
- 4 rounds: 10 jumping lunges each side
- 3 rounds: 20 burpees, 20 air squats, 20 plank up-downs
- 3 rounds: 35 calf raises

DAY 224

Original Session: Warm up - 5 minutes: 30 seconds fast/30 seconds slow assault bike, then 2 rounds: 10 lunges each side, 10 push-ups, 5 jumping pull-ups, instep stretch, dislocates, pigeon stretch. 5 rounds: 5 bent over row (5 seconds down, 1 second at the bottom, 5 seconds up) up in weight each round. Then, with a partner complete: 1,000 meter row, 60 burpee box jump overs, 120 kettlebell swings, 1,000 meter row, 60 burpee pull-ups, 120 ball slams, 1,000 meter row.

Home Edition:

- 5 minutes: 30 seconds high knees, 30 seconds calf raises
- 2 rounds: 10/10 lunges, 10 push-ups, 5 jump squats
- 100 jumping jacks, 30 sumo squats, 60 inchworm walkouts, 30 mountain climbers, 100 jumping jacks

DAY 225

Original Session: Warm up - 3 minute jump rope, then 3 rounds: 5 ring rows, 5 box jumps, sumo stretch, dislocates. Toes to bar technique work. Then, against a 4 minute clock: 25 toes to bar, 50 double unders, (150 singles) 15 squat cleans, 25 toes to bar.

Home Edition:

- 3 minutes jumping jacks
- 3 rounds: 5 wide grip push-ups, 5 air squats
- 25 double leg raises, 50 tuck jumps, 50 spiderman mountain climbers, 25 single leg glute bridge pulses right, 25 single leg glute bridge pulses left

DAY 226

Original Session: Warm up - 2 rounds: 10 lunges each side, 5 pull-ups, 10 push-ups, 5 box jumps. With a partner, complete: 40 box jumps, 200 meter run, 60 deadlifts, 200 meter run, 80 dumbbell thrusters, 200 meter run, 100 kettlebell swings. Then, 3 rounds of the following battle rope complex: 20 slams, 20 alternating, 20 side to side, 20 jumping jacks.

Home Edition:

- 100 burpees
- 100 sit-ups
- 100 air squats
- 100 calf raises

DAY 227

Original Session: Warm up - 3 rounds: 4 gym sprints, 10 squats, dislocates, instep stretch. With a partner, complete as many repetitions of the following in 20 minutes: 12 kettlebell swings, 12 toes to bar, 12 kettlebell snatch, 12 ground to overhead, 12 bar over burpees, 250 meter run. Finally, complete 3 rounds of parallel bar swing throughs.

Home Edition:

- 3 rounds: 1 minute high knees, 10 air squats
- In 20 minutes, complete as many of the following as possible: 12 plank jacks, 12 v-up sit-ups, 12 overhead squats, 12 tricep dips, 12 marching glute bridges
- 3 rounds of one minute plank hold

DAY 228

Original Session: Warm up - 5 minutes 30 seconds fast/30 seconds slow assault bike. Then 2 rounds: 5 push-ups, 5 air squats, 5 box jumps. Then, work to a heavy back squat. Then, 4 rounds: 3 back squats at 70% of maximum effort, one minute all out row, rest 2 minutes. Finish with 3 rounds for time of: 21-15-9 repetitions of: wall balls, pull-ups, ground to overheads.

Home Edition:

- 5 minute jog around your block or accumulate 5 minutes of: high knees, jumping jacks, butt kickers, heisman, jog in place
- 2 rounds: 5 diamond push-ups, 5 side lunges each side, 5 air squats
- 4 rounds: 10 frog jumps
- 3 rounds: 21-15-9 repetitions of: plank up downs, stance jacks, scissor kick abs

DAY 229

Original Session: Warm up - 5 minutes 30 seconds fast/30 seconds slow assault bike. Work to one rep max power clean. At the top of each minute for 6 minutes: 2 power cleans at 70% of maximum effort. Then, complete as many rounds as possible in 20 minutes of: kettlebell snatch, box jumps, back squats, assault bike or row sprint (40 seconds work/20 seconds rest).

Home Edition:

- 3 minutes jumping jacks
- 6 rounds: 30 seconds - 1 minute handstand hold
- 6 rounds: 30 seconds - 1 minute wall sit hold
- As many rounds as possible in 20 minutes of: 10 spiderman mountain climbers, 10 reverse lunges each side, 10 lateral plank walks, 10 single leg deadlifts each side, 10 front kicks each side, 10 side kicks each side, 10 sit-ups

DAY 230

Original Session: Warm up - 2 rounds: 1 minute assault bike, 10 lunges each side, 5 box jumps, 5 pull-ups. Then, work to a heavy 1 rep max front squat. Next, perform 3 rounds of 3 front squats, 100 meter sprint, walk back is the rest. Finish with 6 rounds: 250 meter row sprint.

Home Edition:

- 2 rounds: 1 minute sprint in place, 10 side lunges each side, 5 stance jacks, 5 push-ups
- 50-40-30-20-10 repetitions of: air squats, sit-ups, side plank dips, (½ repetitions one side, ½ repetitions other side) inchworm to down dog, calf raises

DAY 231

Original Session: Warm up - 2 minute assault bike, then 2 rounds: 10 overhead squats, 5 box jumps, 5 pull-ups, sumo stretch, dislocates. Snatch skill technique, muscle up technique. Then as many rounds as possible in 7 minutes of: 10 power snatch, 3 muscle ups. 3 rounds, 45 seconds each: hollow hold, superman hold.

Home Edition:

- 2 minute jog in place
- 2 rounds: 10 overhead squats, 5 jumping lunges each side, 5 push-ups
- Complete as many rounds as possible in 7 minutes of: 3 wall walks, 10 tuck jumps, 5 wide grip push-ups
- 3 rounds, 45 seconds each: hollow hold, superman hold

DAY 232

Original Session: Warm up - 500 meter run, then 2 rounds: 10 air squats, 10 kettlebell swings, 10 push-ups, instep stretch, sump stretch. Then, 6 rounds: 10 v-sit double kettlebell press. Then, as many repetitions of cleans as possible in 7 minutes. Finish with as many row calories as possible in 7 minutes.

Home Edition:

- 5 minute jog around your block
- 2 rounds: 10 air squats, 10 side lunges each side, 10 push-ups
- 6 rounds: 10 floor switch kicks
- In 7 minutes, complete as many burpees possible
- In 7 minutes, complete as many sit-up variation of your choice possible

DAY 233

Original Session: Warm up - 1 gym length each: kick walks, lunges, knee pulls, karaoke walks. 7 rounds: tabata air squats (20 seconds on, 10 seconds bottom hold). As many rounds as possible in 20 minutes of: 200 meter sandbag run, 6 sandbag cleans, 8 sandbag deadlifts, 10 double burpee overs. Finish with 3 rounds: 8 dumbbell front lift, 8 dumbbell side lift, 8 dumbbell curl.

Home Edition:

- 1 minute each: toe touches, alternating quad stretch, alternating knee pulls, high knees, butt kickers
- 7 rounds of tabata air squats (20 seconds squats, 10 seconds hold at bottom = 1 round)
- As many rounds as possible in 20 minutes of: 20 jumping jacks, 6 plank hops, 8 spiderman mountain climbers, 10 jumping lunges each side
- 3 rounds: 10 tricep dips, 10 v-up sit-ups, 10 flutter kicks

DAY 234

Original Session: Warm up - 2 rounds: 30 second jump rope, 5 lunges each side, 5 ring rows, 10 push-ups, medicine ball shoulder stretch, instep stretch. 5 rounds: 4 negative pull-ups, 4 tricep dips. Then, 4 rounds: 15 second dragonfly hold, 30 second handstand hold. 100 double unders (or 300 singles) directly into: 2 rounds of 30 calorie row, 15 toes to bar. Finish with 100 double unders or 300 singles.

Home Edition:

- 2 rounds: 30 seconds jump rope in place, 5 lunges each side, 5 tricep dips, 10 push-ups
- 5 rounds: 4 slow count push-ups, 4 one leg tricep dips each side
- 4 rounds: 30 second hollow hold, 30 second superman hold
- 5 minute as many jumping jacks as possible

DAY 235

Original Session: Warm up - 3 minute assault bike, then 2 rounds: 5 push-ups, 10 air squats, instep stretch. Then, 3 rounds: 10 shoulder to overhead, up in weight each round, 1 minute gym length sprints. Next, 3 rounds: 10 deadlifts, up in weight each round, 1 minute gym length sprints. Finish with 2 rounds: 15 hand release push-ups,10 double kettlebell row, 20 russian twists.

Home Edition:

- 3 minute jog in place
- 2 rounds: 5 push-ups, 10 air squats
- 3 rounds: 10 single leg reach and jumps each side, 1 minute sprint in place
- 3 rounds: 20 tuck jumps, 1 minute sprint in place
- 2 rounds: 15 hand release push-ups, 10 tricep dips, 20 unweighted Russian twists

DAY 236

TAKE YOUR VICTORIES, WHATEVER THEY MAY BE, CHERISH THEM, USE THEM, BUT DON'T SETTLE FOR THEM. — MIA HAMM

Original Session: Warm up - 500 meter row, then 2 rounds: 2 wall walks, 5 single leg kettlebell deadlifts each side, 8 medicine ball cleans. Handstand technique work. Finish with as many repetitions possible in 12 minutes of: 55 deadlifts, 55 wall balls, 55 calorie row, 55 push-ups.

Home Edition:

- 4 minute jog in place or accumulate 4 minutes of: jumping jacks, high knees, butt kickers, mummy kicks
- 2 rounds: 5 single leg deadlifts each side, 8 air squats
- Practice handstand holds
- Against a 12 minute clock: 55 unweighted deadlifts, 55 air squats, 55 mountain climbers, 55 push-ups

DAY 237

Original Session: Warm up - 500 meter row, 5 box step ups each side, 10 air squats, 10 ring rows, instep stretch. Then, work to rope climb or progression of choice. 4 rounds: 10 Bulgarian split squats each side, 1 rope climb. Finish with burpee fest of: 7 calorie row buy in, 1 burpee. At the top of each minute until failure: 7 calorie row, add one burpee.

Home Edition:

- 3 minute jumping jacks
- 2 rounds: 10 air squats, 10 reverse lunges each side
- 4 rounds: 2 wall walks, 10 side lunges each side
- Burpee fest: start with one burpee and at the top of each minute until failure, add one burpee

DAY 238

Original Session: Warm up - 400 meter run, then 2 rounds: 5 hang power cleans, 7 strict presses, 9 front squats. Then, 5 rounds: 30 second handstand hold, 30 second squat hold, 30 seconds rest. Next, 30 hang power cleans, 15 weighted sit-ups, 9 box jumps, 2 air squats. Followed by 2 rounds of: 15 hang power cleans, 10 sit-ups, 6 box jumps, 2 air squats. Then, 3 rounds of: 10 hang power clean, 5 sit-ups, 3 box jumps, 2 air squats. Finish with 8 rounds of: hollow hold/superman hold tabata (20 seconds on/10 seconds rest).

Home Edition:

- 5 rounds: 30 seconds handstand hold, 30 seconds wall sit
- 30 plank up-downs, 15 sit-ups, 9 frog jumps, 2 air squats
- 2 rounds: 15 plank up-downs, 9 sit-ups, 6 frog jumps, 2 air squats, 3 rounds: 10 plank up-downs, 5 sit-ups, 3 frog jumps, 2 air squats
- 8 rounds: Abs tabata: alternate between hollow hold and superman hold (20 seconds work, 10 seconds rest)

DAY 239

Original Session: Warm up - 2 rounds: 1 minute assault bike, 10 kettlebell swings, 10 lunges each side, 10 push-ups, instep stretch. Work to a heavy deadlift. Then complete: 21-15-9 repetitions of: deadlifts, pull-ups, 400 meter run. Finish with 3 rounds of: 10 v-up sit-ups, 5 penguins each side.

Home Edition:

- 2 rounds: 1 minute jog in place, 10 sit-ups, 10 lunges each side, 10 push-ups
- 21-15-9 repetitions of: burpees, tuck jumps, flutter kicks
- 3 rounds: 10 bicycle crunches, 5 penguins each side

DAY 240

Original Session: Warm up - 2 rounds: 5 hang cleans, 5 lunges each side, 5 box jumps, pigeon stretch, dislocates. Squat clean/push jerk technique work. 5 rounds: 1 clean & jerk at 90% of maximum effort. Then, as many rounds as possible in 12 minutes of: 10 kettlebell front rack lunges, 10 Turkish get ups, 10 burpee box jumps.

Home Edition:

- 5 minute jog around your block or 5 minutes jog in place
- 2 rounds: 5 lunges each side, 5 jump squats
- 5 rounds: 10 front kicks each side, 10 side kicks each side, 20 standing oblique crunch each side
- Against a 12 minute clock, as many rounds as possible of: 10 reverse lunges each side, 5 lateral plank walks each side, 10 glute bridge walk outs

DAY 241

Original Session: Warm up - 5 minutes 30 seconds fast/30 seconds moderate assault bike. 5 rounds: 5 pull-ups, 10 push-ups. Then, a 500 meter row followed by 3 rounds: 15 thrusters, 75 double unders / 150 singles. Finish with a 500 meter row. Lastly, complete 3 rounds maximum distance farmer carry.

Home Edition:

- 5 minutes of: high knees, jog in place, butt kickers, heisman, mummy kicks
- 5 rounds: 5 wide grip push-ups, 10 spiderman mountain climbers
- 25 burpees, 45 air squats, 150 jumping jacks
- Accumulate a total of 5 minutes in plank hold of choice

DAY 242

Original Session: Warm up - At the top of each minute for 5 minutes: 5 push-ups, 5 air squats, 1 gym length sprint. For time: 21-18-15-12-9-6-3 repetitions of: thrusters and burpees.

Home Edition:

- At the top of each minute for 5 minutes: 5 push-ups, 5 air squats, 10 high knees
- 21-18-15-12-9-6-3 repetitions of: unweighted thrusters and burpees

DAY 243

Original Session: Warm up - 2 rounds: 1 minute assault bike, 10 lunges each side, 5 pull-ups, 5 box jumps, pigeon stretch, instep. For time: 200 meter run, 80 air squats, 200 meter run, 60 overhead kettlebell swings, 200 meter run, 40 ball slams, 200 meter run, 20 deadlifts, 200 meter run, 10 pull-ups.

Home Edition:

- Pick your poison: 300 burpees, 3 mile run, or 20 minutes maximum jumping jacks

DAY 244

Original Session: Warm up - 3 minute row, then 2 rounds: 10 back squats, 10 good mornings, 10 push-ups, 3 wall walks. Then work to a heavy set of 3 back squats. At the top of each minute for 20 minutes, perform 3 back squats at 70-80% of maximum effort, 8 hand release push-ups. Finish with a heavy prowler pull relay.

Home Edition:

- 3 minute jog in place
- 2 rounds: 10 air squats, 10 unweighted good mornings, 10 push-ups, 3 wall walks
- At the top of each minute for 20 minutes: 3 jump squats, 8 hand release push-ups
- Finish with max plank hold for time (shoot for 5 minutes or more)

DAY 245

YOUR HEALTH ACCOUNT, YOUR BANK ACCOUNT, THEY'RE THE SAME THING. THE MORE YOU PUT IN, THE MORE YOU CAN TAKE OUT. EXERCISE IS KING AND NUTRITION IS QUEEN. TOGETHER YOU HAVE A KINGDOM. — JACK LALANNE

Original Session: Warm up - 2 rounds: 1 minute assault bike, 5 squat cleans, 5 front squats, 5 push presses, dislocates. Then, complete 3 rounds of: 8 squat cleans, 400 meter run, 90 seconds rest. Next, complete 3 rounds of: gym length overhead kettlebell carry, 30 calorie row, 90 seconds rest. Finally, complete 3 rounds of: 15 second dragonfly hold, 10 tricep dips, 5/5 kettlebell cross body slashes, 5/5 halos, 10 reverse fly.

Home Edition:

- 2 rounds: 1 minute jumping jacks, 5 side lunges each side, 5 air squats, 5 push-ups
- 3 rounds: 8 squat jacks, 40 mountain climbers
- 3 rounds: 20 hands overhead reverse lunges, 40 plank jacks
- 3 rounds: 15 second hollow hold, 10 tricep dips, 10 russian twists, 15 second superman hold

DAY 246

Original Session: Warm up - 500 meter row, then 2 rounds of: 10 goblet squats, 10 push-ups, dislocates, pigeon stretch. Complete 5 rounds of: Max pull-ups, rest 30 seconds, max bench press, rest 90 seconds. Then alternating repetitions of: 3-6-9-12-15 - burpees and 15-12-9-6-3 front squats.

Home Edition:

- 2 rounds: 10 air squats, 10 push-ups, 5 lunges each side
- 5 rounds: maximum handstand hold, max single leg bridge hold each side, max plank hold
- 3-6-9-12-15 burpees alternating with 15-12-9-6-3 air squats (3 burpees, 15 air squats - 6 burpees, 12 air squats, 9 burpees, 9 air squats. . . until you reach 15 burpees, 3 air squats)

DAY 247

Original Session: Warm up - 2 rounds: 200 meter run, 10 push-ups, 10 air squats, 10 jumping squats, 10 jump rope, instep stretch, dislocates, pigeon stretch. Double under skill practice, then 10 minutes: 30 second double unders, 30 second rest. Then, 12 minutes to complete as many repetitions as possible of: 5/5 barbell lunges, 7 push presses, 9 pull-ups. Finish with 30-20-10 repetitions of: Weighted sit-ups, L-sit holds, butterfly sit-ups.

Home Edition:

- 2 rounds: 1 minute each: high knees, push-up to down dog, air squats, jump rope in place
- 10 minute Jump rope practice if you have a jump rope, if not, maximum jumping jacks in 10 minutes
- As many rounds as possible in 12 minutes: 5 reverse lunges each side, 7 push-ups, 9 straight leg sit-ups
- 30-20-10 repetitions of: flutter kicks, glute bridge walk outs, scissor kicks

DAY 248

Original Session: Warm up - At the top of every minute for 5 minutes: 5 ball slams, 5 kettlebell swings, 5 box jumps. Then, 3 rounds of: 8 deadlifts up in weight each round, 3 box jumps, 400 meter run, 90 seconds rest. Then, 3 rounds of: 8 front squats, 20 seconds knees to chest hold, 90 seconds jump rope, 90 seconds rest. Finisher: 500 meter row sprint, rest 2 minutes, 250 meter row sprint.

Home Edition:

- At the top of each minute for 5 minutes, perform 5 unweighted thrusters, 5 air squats, 5 unweighted good mornings
- 3 rounds of: 8 plank shoulder taps, 8 in and out abs, 1 minute sprint in place
- 3 rounds of: 8 single leg reach and jumps each side, 30 seconds boat hold
- Finisher: 5 minutes max burpees

DAY 249

Original Session: Warm up - 2 rounds: 1 minute assault bike, 10 push-ups, 10 air squats, 5 jumping pull-ups, sumo stretch. 5 rounds: 3 push presses, 1 rope climb. Then, 4 rounds: 250 meter row, then against a 2 minute cock, 5 ground to overheads, 5 burpee box jumps. Finish with 3 rounds 10/10 kettlebell Russian twists.

Home Edition:

- 1 minute jog in place, 2 rounds: 10 push-ups, 10 air squats, 5 sit-ups
- 5 rounds: 10 side plank dips each side, 5 tuck jumps
- 30 burpees
- 3 rounds 10/10 unweighted Russian twists

DAY 250

> *HE WHO CANNOT OBEY HIMSELF WILL BE COMMANDED. THAT IS THE NATURE OF LIVING CREATURES. — FRIEDRICH NIETZSCHE*

Original Session: Warm up - 2 rounds: 5 squat cleans, 5 box jumps, 5 lunges each side, pigeon stretch, sumo stretch. Work to a heavy clean & jerk. Then at the top of each minute for 6 minutes: 1-2 clean & jerk. 3 rounds for time: 30 wall balls, 20 kettlebell snatch, 10 pull-ups.

Home Edition:

- 2 rounds: 5 squat jacks, 5 high jumps, 5 side lunges each side
- 6 rounds: Max handstand hold
- 3 rounds: 30 air squats, 20 flutter kicks, 10 diamond push-ups

DAY 251

Original Session: Warm up - 2 rounds: 250 meter row, 5 lunges each side, 5 box jumps, 10 kettlebell swings. Then, 5 rounds: 3 deadlifts up in weight each round. For time: 50 calorie assault bike, 15 kettlebell swings, 10 box jumps, 40 calorie bike, 15 kettlebell swings, 10 box jumps, 30 calorie bike, 15 kettlebell swings, 10 box jumps, 20 calorie bike, 15 kettlebell swings, 10 box jumps, 10 calorie bike, 15 kettlebell swings, 10 box jumps

Home Edition:

- 2 rounds: 1 minute high knees, 5 lunges each side, 5 jump squats
- For time: 50 air squats, 15 calf raises, 10 spiderman mountain climbers, 40 air squats: 15 in and out abs, 10 glute bridge walk outs, 30 air squats, 15 plank jacks, 10 tricep dips, 20 air squats, 15 wide grip push-ups, 10 straight leg sit-ups, 10 air squats, 15 push-up to down dog, 10 single leg deadlift each side

DAY 252

Original Session: Warm up - 2 rounds: 30 second jump rope, 3 wall walks, 10 air squats, instep stretch. Work to a heavy split jerk. Then, 6 rounds: 2 split jerks at 80% of maximum effort. At the top of each minute for 21 minutes: 10 calorie row, 6 burpee box jumps, 15 slam balls. Finish with 2 rounds: 15 curl to press, 15 sit-ups, 15 push-ups, 15 Russian twists.

Home Edition:

- 2 rounds: 30 seconds jump rope in place, 3 wall walks, 10 air squats
- At the top of each minute for 21 minutes: 30 second sprint in place, 6 burpees, 15 air squats
- 2 rounds: 15 tricep dips, 15 sit-ups, 15 push-ups, 15 Russian twists

DAY 253

Original Session: Warm up - 400 meter run, then 2 rounds: 10 goblet squats, 10 kettlebell swings, 5 pull-ups, sumo stretch. 4 rounds: max pull-ups, max dips, rest 2 minutes. Finish with: 800 meter run, then 3 rounds: 30 wall balls, 15 toes to bar, 800 meter run. Accumulate 90 seconds in an L-sit.

Home Edition:

- 5 minutes jog around your block or jog in place
- 2 rounds: 10 air squats, 10 push-ups, 5 squat jacks
- 4 rounds: max handstand hold, max tricep dips
- 3 rounds: 30 air squats, 15 v-up-sit-ups
- 50 burpees

DAY 254

Original Session: Warm up - 2 rounds: 1 minute assault bike, 5 deadlifts, 5 Romanian deadlifts, 5 lunges each side, 5 push-ups, sumo stretch, instep stretch. Work to a heavy deadlift, then 5 rounds of: 5 bodyweight deadlifts, 10 wall balls, 1 minute airdyne sprint. Finish with 3 rounds of 10/10 Russian twist, 10 weighted sit-ups, 10 superman holds.

Home Edition:

- 2 rounds: 1 minute jumping jacks, 5 one leg deadlifts each side, 5 Romanian deadlifts, 5 lunges each side. 5 rounds: 30 second handstand hold, 10 air squats, one minute sprint in place.
- 3 rounds: 10/10 Russian twist, 10 straight leg sit-ups, 10 hollow rocks, 10 superman holds

DAY 255

Original Session: Warm up - At the top of each minute for 5 minutes: 5 push-ups, 5 air squats, 5 box jumps. Then, 3 rounds of: 5 push presses, up in weight each round, 400 meter run, 90 seconds rest. 3 rounds: 5 power cleans, 3 box jumps, 2 minute row, (30 seconds moderate/30 seconds sprint) 90 seconds rest. 3 rounds battle rope complex: 20 slams, 20/20 alternate, 20/20 side to side, 20 jumping jacks.

Home Edition:

- At the top of each minute for 5 minutes: 5 push-ups, 5 air squats, 5 tuck jumps
- 3 rounds: 5 pike push-ups, 2 minute sprint in place
- 3 rounds: 20 plank jacks, 2 minute jumping jacks
- 3 rounds: 20 flutter kicks, 20 scissor kicks, 20 bicycle crunches

DAY 256

> *IF YOU TAKE TIME TO REALIZE WHAT YOUR DREAM IS AND WHAT YOU REALLY WANT IN LIFE — NO MATTER WHAT IT IS, WHETHER IT'S SPORTS OR IN OTHER FIELDS — YOU HAVE TO REALIZE THAT THERE IS ALWAYS WORK TO DO, AND YOU WANT TO BE THE HARDEST WORKING PERSON IN WHATEVER YOU DO, AND YOU PUT YOURSELF IN A POSITION TO BE SUCCESSFUL. AND YOU HAVE TO HAVE A PASSION ABOUT WHAT YOU DO. — STEPHEN CURRY*

Original Session: Warm up - 2 rounds: 200 meter run, 10 kettlebell swings, 10 lunges each side, 10 jumping pull-ups, instep stretch. Work to a heavy squat clean. Then, at the top of each minute for 7 minutes: 2 squat cleans at 80-90% of maximum effort. For time: 500 meter row, 50 dumbbell snatches, 50 calorie assault bike, 30 dumbbell snatches, 500 meter row, 20 dumbbell snatches, 50 calorie assault bike, 10 dumbbell snatches.

Home Edition:

- 2 rounds: 1 minute each: high knees, butt kickers, side to side lunges, jumping jacks
- At the top of each minute for 7 minutes: 5 burpees
- 25 lateral plank walks each side, 50 side kicks each side, 50 front kicks each side, 50 plank up downs, 25 inchworm to push-up

DAY 257

Original Session: Warm up - 10 push-ups, 5 pull-ups, 10 air squats, dislocates, sumo stretch. Then, 5 rounds: 5 bench presses up in weight each round, 10/10 kettlebell rows. 3 rounds: tabata stations - 40 seconds on/20 seconds rest: ground to overhead, box jumps, kettlebell swings, burpees, 1 minute rest between rounds.

Home Edition:

- 10 push-ups, 5 straight leg sit-ups, 10 air squats
- 5 rounds: 3 wall walks, 10 hollow rocks
- 3 rounds, 40 seconds on/20 seconds rest: convict squats, tuck jumps, burpees, reverse lunges

DAY 258

Original Session: Warm up - 3 rounds: 30 second jump rope, 5 burpees, instep stretch, pigeon stretch. Work to a heavy set of 5 strict presses. Then 5 rounds: 5 strict press, 5 strict pull-ups. For time: 50 calorie row, 50 box jump overs, 50 burpees.

Home Edition:

- 3 rounds: 30 second jumping jacks, 5 burpees
- 5 rounds: 5 pike push-ups
- 50 froggers, 50 twisting crunches, 50 burpees

DAY 259

Original Session: Warm up - 500 meter row, 2 rounds: 10 back squat, 10 kettlebell swing, 10 ring row. Work to a heavy back squat. 4 rounds: 3 back squat at 70-80% of maximum effort. 4 rounds: as many rounds as possible in 3 minutes: 7 muscle ups, 21 wall balls, 1 minute rest between rounds. 3 rounds: 100 meter heavy farmer carry, 5 toes to bar.

Home Edition:

- 4 minute jog around your block or accumulate 4 minutes of: jog in place, high knees, butt kickers, side to side lunges
- 2 rounds: 10 air squats, 10 tricep dips
- 4 rounds: as many rounds as possible in 7 minutes of: 7 handstand push-ups, 21 air squats.
- 3 rounds: max plank hold, 5 v-up sit-ups

DAY 260

Original Session: Warm up - 5 minutes: 30 seconds moderate/30 seconds fast assault bike, instep stretch, foam roll, dislocates. 7 rounds: 3 power cleans, up in weight each round. With a partner, complete: 1,000 meter row, 50 dumbbell push presses, 50 pull-ups, 1,000 meter row, 25 burpees, 25 thrusters.

Home Edition:

- 5 minute jog around your block or accumulate 5 minutes of jogging in place, jumping jacks, high knees, butt kickers
- 7 rounds: 5 hand release push ups
- 30 burpees, 25 overhead squats, 25 push-ups, 25 straight leg sit-ups, 30 burpees, 25 side plank dips each side

DAY 261

Original Session: Warm up - 30 seconds each: jump rope, air squats, push-ups, dislocates. 5 rounds: 6 deadlifts, up in weight each round. For time: 65 calorie assault bike, 3 minutes rest, then 3 rounds: 10 ground to overhead, 15 toes to bar, 30 double unders (90 singles).

Home Edition:

- 30 seconds each: jump rope in place, air squats, push-ups
- 5 rounds: 30 second wall sit hold
- 60 air squats
- 3 rounds: 10 thrusters, 15 v-up sit-ups, 30 single leg reach and jumps each side

DAY 262

Original Session: Warm up - 2 rounds: 1 minute assault bike, 10 deadlifts, 10 front squats, 5 hang squat cleans, instep stretch. 5 rounds: 3 hang squat cleans, up in weight each round. Then, as many rounds as possible in 7 minutes of: 7 burpees, 7 dumbbell thruster, 7 box jumps.

Home Edition:

- 2 rounds: 1 minute jog in place, 10 Romanian deadlifts, 10 air squats, 5 sit-ups
- 5 rounds: 10 jumping lunges each side
- As many rounds as possible in 7 minutes: 7 burpees, 7 unweighted thrusters, 7 jump squats

DAY 263

Original Session: Warm up - 3 rounds: 5 lunges each side, 10 jumping jacks, 5 hollow hang holds, scarecrow, instep stretch, pigeon stretch, dislocates. With a partner: 200 meter run, 100 squats, 100 dumbbell push press, 200 meter run, 60 wall balls, 60 sandbag get ups, 40 push-ups, 40 pull-ups.

Home Edition:

- 3 rounds: 5 reverse lunges each side, 10 jumping jacks, 5 hollow rocks
- 2 minute jog in place, 50 air squats, 50 unweighted thrusters, 2 minute jog in place, 30 side squats each side, 30 plank walk outs, 20 push-ups, 20 glute bridge walk outs

DAY 264

WE DON'T EVEN KNOW HOW STRONG WE ARE UNTIL WE ARE FORCED TO BRING THAT HIDDEN STRENGTH FORWARD. — ISABEL ALLENDE

Original Session: Warm up - 2 rounds: 200 meter run, 10 back squats, 10 lunges each side, 5 box jumps, pigeon stretch. Work to a heavy back squat. Then, 5 rounds: 3 back squats, 100 meter sprint, walk back is rest. Next, as many rounds as possible in 8 minutes of: 21 overhead kettlebell swings, 15 wall balls, 9 box jumps. Finish with 2 rounds battle rope complex: 20 slams, 20/20 side to side, 20/20 alternate, 20 jumping jacks.

Home Edition:

- 2 rounds: 1 minute high knees, 10 air squats, 10 side lunges each side, 5 jump squats.
- 5 rounds: 3 air squats, 30 second sprint in place
- As many rounds as possible in 8 minutes of: 21 overhead squats, 15 froggers, 9 jump squats
- 5 minute max butterfly sit ups

DAY 265

Original Session: Warm up - At the top of each minute for 5 minutes: 5 push press, 5 air squats, 5 box jumps, dislocates. 5 rounds: 10 dumbbell curl to press, 10/10 kettlebell bent over row, 90 second rest. 500 meter row, then: 4 rounds: 5 squat cleans, 10 pull-ups, 5 burpee box jumps. Finish with a 500 meter row.

Home Edition:

- At the top of each minute for 5 minutes: 5 push-ups, 5 air squats, 5 jumping jacks
- 5 rounds: 10 floor switch kicks, 10 side plank dips each side
- 50 jumping jacks, then 4 rounds: 10 flutter kicks, 10 burpees
- Finish with 50 stance jacks

DAY 266

Original Session: Warm up - Kettlebell swing and back squat ladder: 15-12-9-12-6, med ball shoulders, dislocates. 5 rounds: 5-10 strict pull-ups, 5-10 push-ups. Then, 21 deadlifts, 40 calorie assault bike, 80 double unders, (160 singles) 15 deadlifts, 30 calorie assault bike, 60 double unders, (120 singles) 9 deadlifts, 20 calorie assault bike, 40 double unders (80 singles).

Home Edition:

- 15-12-9-12-6 repetitions of: plank jacks, calf raises
- 5 rounds: 5-10 handstand push-ups, 10 plank up-downs
- 21 straight leg sit-ups, 20 burpees, 15 tuck jumps, 20 in and out abs, 9 unweighted man makers, 20 star jumps

DAY 267

Original Session: Warm up - 2 rounds: 1 minute assault bike, 5 hang power cleans, 5 box jumps, 5 lunges each side, sumo stretch. Work to a heavy power clean. Then as many rounds as possible in 12 minutes of: 200 meter row, 15 kettlebell swings, 10 wall balls, 5 toes to bar. Finish with 2 rounds: 20 butterfly sit-ups, 10/10 Russian twists, 1 minute plank.

Home Edition:

- 2 rounds: 1 minute jog in place, 5 jump squats, 5 lunges each side
- As many rounds as possible in 12 minutes of: 15 burpees, 10 diamond push-ups, 5 tricep dips
- 2 rounds: 20 butterfly sit-ups, 10/10 Russian twists, 1 minute plank

DAY 268

Original Session: Warm up - 500 meter row, then 2 rounds: 5 push-ups, 10 walking lunges, 5 jumping pull-ups, instep stretch, dislocates. Work to a heavy front squat, then at the top of each minute for 5 minutes, 5 front squats at 70% of maximum effort, 2 high box jumps. Finish with 50-40-30-20-10 calorie row, thrusters (thrusters ½ repetitions).

Home Edition:

- 5 minute jog around your block or accumulate 5 minutes of: high knees, butt kickers, mummy kicks, heisman, jog in place
- 2 rounds: 5 push-ups, 10 walking lunges, 5 air squats
- 50-40-30-20-10 repetitions of: air squats, sit-ups, spiderman mountain climbers

DAY 269

Original Session: Warm up - 5 minutes, 30 seconds moderate/30 seconds fast assault bike. 6 rounds: 8 dumbbell seated military press, 8 strict pull-ups. For time: 1,000 meter row, 35 burpees, 800 meter row. Finish with 2 rounds: 20 sit-ups, 20 Russian twist, 1 minute plank

Home Edition:

- 5 minutes - 30 second jog in place, 30 second standing quad stretch
- 6 rounds: 8 hand release push-ups, 8 plank shoulder taps each side
- 70 air squats, 35 burpees, 25 side lunges each side
- 2 rounds: 20 sit-ups, 20 Russian twist each side, 1 minute elevated side plank (30 seconds each side)

DAY 270

> *THE REAL MAN SMILES IN TROUBLE, GATHERS STRENGTH FROM DISTRESS, AND GROWS BRAVE BY REFLECTION. — THOMAS PAINE*

Original Session: Warm up - 3 rounds: 30 second jump rope, 10 back squat, 10 push-ups, instep stretch, sumo stretch. Work to a heavy back squat. Then, 4 rounds: 3 back squats at 70% of maximum effort, 3 box jumps. Next, 4 rounds: 25 wall balls, 10 toes to bar. Finish with a 1,000 meter row for time.

Home Edition:

- 3 rounds: 30 second stance jacks, 10 pausing air squats, 10 push-ups
- 4 rounds: 1 minute wall sit hols
- 4 rounds: 25 front kicks each side, 10 v-up sit-ups
- 1 minute each: flutter kicks, scissor kicks, superman hold, hollow hold, plank

DAY 271

> *THE ONLY THING THAT EVER SAT ITS WAY TO SUCCESS WAS A HEN. — SARAH BROWN*

Original Session: Warm up - 3 minute assault bike, then 2 rounds: 10 push presses, 10 ring rows, dislocates. 5 rounds: 5 push press up in weight each round, 10/10 dumbbell row. Finish with 3 rounds: 400 meter run, 21 overhead kettlebell swings, 12 pull-ups.

Home Edition:

- 3 minute jog around your block or accumulate 3 minutes of: jog in place, high knees, butt kickers
- 2 rounds: 10 push-ups, 10 tricep dips
- 3 rounds: 20 burpees, 21 tuck jumps, 12 marching glute bridges

DAY 272

Original Session: Warm up - 10 kettlebell swings, 10 air squats, instep stretch. Work to a heavy deadlift. Then, 21-15-9 repetitions of: deadlifts, toes to bar, double unders (triple repetitions for singles). Finish with 3 rounds, 30 seconds each: handstand hold, rest, hollow hold, rest.

Home Edition:

- 2 rounds: 10 reverse lunges each side, 10 air squats
- 21-15-9 repetitions of: unweighted thrusters, v-up sit-ups, jumping jacks (triple number of repetitions for jumping jacks)
- 3 rounds: 30 seconds handstand hold, 30 seconds hollow hold

DAY 273

Original Session: Warm up - 5 jumping pull-ups, 5 box jumps, 5/5 lunges, dislocates, instep stretch. Work to a heavy clean & jerk. Then, at the top of each minute for 6 minutes: 1 squat clean, 1 front squat, 1 jerk. Finish with as many rounds as possible in 12 minutes of: 20 overhead plate walking lunges, 5/5 dumbbell snatch, 10 box jumps.

Home Edition:

- 2 rounds: 5 inchworm to push-ups, 5 jump squats
- At the top of each minute for 6 minutes: 5 burpees
- As many rounds as possible in 12 minutes of: 20 overhead walking lunges, 10 ski down abs, 10 twisting crunches

DAY 274

Original Session: Warm up - 2 rounds: 5 jumping pull-ups, 5 push-ups, 5 box jumps, 5/5 lunges. Then, 5 rounds: 5 strict pull-ups. Next, 4 rounds against a 3 minute clock: 200 meter run, followed by as many rounds as possible of: 15 kettlebell swings, 15 air squats. Finish with 3 rounds of: 10/10 Russian twist, 10 toes to bar, 1 minute plank.

Home Edition:

- 2 rounds: 5 burpees, 5 lunges each side, 5 push-ups
- 5 rounds: 5 handstand push-ups or max handstand hold
- 4 rounds against a 3 minute clock: start with 1 minute sprint in place, then as many rounds as possible of: 15 air squats, 15 unweighted thrusters
- 3 rounds: 20 Russian twist, 10 pike push-ups, 1 minute plank

DAY 275

Original Session: Warm up - 5 minutes: 30 seconds moderate/30 seconds fast assault bike. Work to a heavy deadlift. Then, 20-15-10 repetitions of: deadlift, pull-ups. May substitute 5-3-1 rope climb. Finish with 1 minute plank, 30 seconds hollow hold, 1 minute plank, 30 seconds hollow hold, 1 minute plank

Home Edition:

- 5 minutes: 30 seconds jog in place, 30 seconds calf raises
- 20-15-10 repetitions of: tuck jumps, plyo push-ups, straight leg sit-ups
- 1 minute plank, 30 seconds hollow hold, 1 minute plank, 30 seconds hollow hold, 1 minute plank

DAY 276

Original Session: Warm up - 2 rounds: 1 minute assault bike, 5 back squats, 5 push presses, 5 box jumps, instep stretch, sumo stretch. Work to a heavy back squat. Then, 5 rounds: 3 back squats at 60-70% of maximum effort. Finish with partner: 60-50-40-30-20-10 repetitions of: calorie row, wall balls

Home Edition:

- 2 rounds: 1 minute jog in place, 5 air squats, 5 push-ups, 10 sit-ups
- 5 rounds: 3 glute bridge walk outs
- 60-50-40-30-20-10 repetitions of: plank shoulder taps, squat jacks

DAY 277

Original Session: Warm up - 500 meter row, then 2 rounds: 10 air squat, 10 push-ups, sumo stretch. 3 rounds: 8 overhead squat, up in weight each round, 30 seconds moderate/30 seconds fast row x2, 90 seconds rest between rounds. Then, 3 rounds: 8 ground to overhead, 8 toes to bar, 400 meter run, 90 seconds rest. Finish with 3 rounds heavy prowler push/pull.

Home Edition:

- 3 minute jog around your block or accumulate 3 minutes of: jumping jacks, jog in place, high knees
- 2 rounds: 10 air squats, 10 push-ups
- 8 rounds: 8 jumping lunges each side, 30 seconds sprint in place
- 3 rounds: 8 side step squats each side, 8 v-up sit-ups, 2 minute sprint in place
- Max plank hold (try for at least 5 minutes)

DAY 278

Original Session: Warm up - 10 rounds: Tabata 20 second on/10 seconds rest push-ups, air squats. 3 rounds against a 6 minute clock: 400 meter run, then 10 box jump overs, 7 pull-ups. Finish with 3 rounds: 10 Romanian deadlift.

Home Edition:

- 10 rounds, 20 seconds on, 10 seconds rest: push-ups, air squats (alternate exercise each round for 5 rounds each)
- 3 rounds against a 6 minute clock: 7 burpees, then 10 jump squats, 7 diamond push-ups
- 3 rounds: 10 straight leg deadlift, 10 single leg reach and jump each side, 10 flutter kicks, 10 scissor kicks

DAY 279

WE ACQUIRE THE STRENGTH WE HAVE OVERCOME. — RALPH WALDO EMERSON

Original Session: Warm up - 2 rounds: 30 second jump rope, 5 hand release push-ups, 5 scarecrow, med ball shoulders. 5 rounds: 8 bench presses, up in weight each round, 5 pull-ups. For time: 400 meter run, then: 21-15-9 repetitions of: thrusters, toes to bar. Complete a 400 meter run in between each round.

Home Edition:

- 2 rounds: 30 second jumping jacks, 5 hand release push-ups, 10 toe touches
- 5 rounds: 8 pike push-ups, 10 spiderman mountain climbers
- 30 burpees, then: 21-15-9 repetitions of: tuck jumps, twisting crunches. Complete 20 burpees between each round.

DAY 280

Original Session: Warm up - 5 minute assault bike, hang power clean progression. Work to a heavy hang power clean. Then, 3 rounds: 10 hang power clean, 100 meter sprint, walk back is rest. Next, 3 rounds: 10/10 split Bulgarian lunges, 1 minute assault bike sprint, 1 minute rest. Finish with 3 rounds of: 10 tricep dips, 10 hand release push-ups, 10 bent over rows, 10 weighted sit-ups.

Home Edition:

- 5 minute jog in place
- 3 rounds: 10 stance jacks, one minute sprint in place
- 3 rounds: 20 alternating reverse lunges, 10 tuck jumps
- 3 rounds: 10 floor switch kicks, 10 hand release push-ups, 10 rope climb sit-ups, 10 hollow rocks

DAY 281

Original Session: Warm up - 2 rounds: 200 meter run, 5/5 lunges, 5 front squat, instep stretch, pigeon. 4 rounds: 4 front squat up in weight each round, 50 meter prowler push, 2 minute rest. As many rounds as possible in 6 minutes of: 12 burpee pull-ups, 200 meter run. Rest 3 minutes. Then, as many rounds as possible in 4 minutes of: 8 burpee pull-ups, 200 meter run. Rest 3 minutes. For time, finish with 12 burpee box jumps, 200 meter run, 8 burpee box jumps, 200 meter run.

Home Edition:

- 2 rounds: 1 minute jumping jacks, 5 lunges each side, 5 air squats.
- As many rounds as possible in 6 minutes of: 12 burpees, 1 minute sprint in place
- As many rounds as possible in 4 minutes of: 8 burpees, 30 second sprint in place
- 12 burpees, 50 jumping jacks, 8 burpees, 50 jumping jacks

DAY 282

Original Session: Warm up - 5 minute assault bike. For time: 1 mile run, 100 pull-ups, 200 push-ups, 300 air squats, 1 mile run.

Home Edition:

- Accumulate 5 minutes of: high knees, jog in place, butt kickers, side to side lunges, push-up to down dog
- 1 mile run
- 100 burpees
- 200 push-ups
- 300 air squats
- 1 mile run

DAY 283

Original Session: Warm up - 2 rounds: 1 minute assault bike, 5/5 lunges, 5 deadlift, 5 box jumps, pigeon. Work to a heavy deadlift. Then 6 rounds: 8 deadlifts, up in weight each round, 2 minute assault bike sprint at 70-75 RPM. 2 minute rest.

Home Edition:

- 2 rounds: 1 minute jog in place, 5/5 lungess, 5 air squats
- 6 rounds: 8 diamond push-ups, 20 burpees

DAY 284

> *TODAY AND ONWARDS, I STAND PROUD, FOR THE BRIDGES I'VE CLIMBED, FOR*
> *THE BATTLES I'VE WON, AND FOR THE EXAMPLES I'VE SET, BUT MOST*
> *IMPORTANTLY, FOR THE PERSON I HAVE BECOME. I LIKE WHO I AM NOW,*
> *FINALLY, AT PEACE WITH ME. — HEATHER JAMES*

Original Session: Warm up - 2 rounds: 200 meter run, 5 jumping pull-ups, 5/5 lunges, sumo stretch, dislocates. 5 rounds: 10 dumbbell curl to press, 10 push-ups. As many repetitions as possible in 14 minutes: 200 meter run, 5 ground to overhead, 5 toes to bar, 5 box jumps.

Home Edition:

- 2 rounds: 25 jumping jacks, 5 push-ups, 5/5 reverse lunges
- 5 rounds: 10 single leg glute bridge pulses each side, 10 wide grip push-ups
- Against a 14 minute clock, as many rounds as possible of: 20 tuck jumps, 5 v-up-sit-ups, 10 mountain climbers

DAY 285

Original Session: Warm up - 2 rounds: 5 back squat, 5 push-ups, 5/5 lunges, instep stretch. 5 rounds: 5 back squat, up in weight each round. 40-30-20-10 repetitions of: calorie row, wall balls or ball slams. Maximum effort in plank hold.

Home Edition:

- 2 rounds: 5 air squats, 5 push-ups, 5/5 side lunges
- 5 rounds: 1 minute wall sit hold, 30 seconds superman hold
- 40-30-20-10 repetitions of: air squat, butterfly sit-ups
- Accumulate maximum minutes in a plank hold of choice

DAY 286

Original Session: Warm up - 2 minute row, then 3 rounds: 5 push press, 5/5 lunges, 5 jumping pull-ups, dislocates, superman, hollow hold. As many rounds as possible in 20 minutes of: 1 minute overhead hold, 16/16 weighted lunges, 30 second kipping practice. Then, as many rounds as possible in 8 minutes of: partner does 20 wall balls while other rows for calories.

Home Edition:

- 3 minute jog around your block or jog in place
- 3 rounds: 5 push-ups, 5/5 lunges, 30 seconds hollow hold, 30 seconds superman hold
- Against a 20 minute clock, as many rounds as possible of: 1 minute overhead squat hold, 16 lunges each side
- 1 minute each: scissor kicks, bicycle crunches, glute bridge hold, flutter kicks

DAY 287

Original Session: Warm up - 5 minutes: 30 seconds moderate/30 seconds fast assault bike, power clean progression. Next, 5 rounds: 3 power clean, 2 front squat, 1 jerk, up in weight each round. For time: 800 meter run, 20 toes to bar, 400 meter run, 20 pull-ups, 200 meter run, 10 handstand push-ups. Finish with 3 rounds of 45 second flutter kicks.

Home Edition:

- 5 minutes, 30 seconds jog in place, 30 seconds calf raises
- 50 burpees, 20 v-up sit-ups, 30 burpees, 20 diamond push-ups, 20 burpees, 20 spiderman mountain climbers

DAY 288

Original Session: Warm up - 1 minute row, then 2 rounds: 10 air squats, 5 burpees, instep, t-spine foam roll. Work to a heavy front squat, then 3 rounds: 2 front squats at 80-85% of maximum effort. Against a 3 minute clock, 50 calorie assault bike. Against a 6 minute clock, as many rounds as possible of: 10 dumbbell thrusters, 5 pull-ups. 3 minute rest. Against a 5 minute clock, as many rounds as possible of: 10 arms only row pulls, 10 shoulder to overhead.

Home Edition:

- 1 minute jumping jacks, 2 rounds: 10 air squats, 5 burpees
- For 3 minutes: max burpees
- For 6 minutes, as many rounds as possible of: 10 unweighted thrusters, 5 hand release push-ups
- For 5 minutes, as many rounds as possible of 10 floor switch kicks, 10 in and out abs

DAY 289

Original Session: Warm up - 5 minute assault bike, 2 rounds: 5 air squats, 5 jump squats, 10 kettlebell swings, instep stretch, sumo stretch. 3 rounds: 10 sandbag jump squats, 1 minute max assault bike calories, 90 second rest. 3 rounds: 12 kettlebell deadlift, 350 meter row, 90 seconds rest. Finish with 3 rounds: 10 tricep dips, 10 push-ups, 10 Romanian deadlifts, 10 strict toes to bar.

Home Edition:

- 1 minute each: jog in place, high knees, butt kickers, mummy kicks, heisman
- 2 rounds: 5 air squats, 5 jump squats, 5 push-ups
- 3 rounds: 10 stance jacks, 1 minute sprint in place
- 3 rounds: 24 unweighted Romanian deadlift, 10 burpees
- 3 rounds: 10 tricep dips, 10 push-ups, 10 v-up sit-ups

DAY 289

Original Session: Warm up - 400 meter run, then 2 rounds of: 8 back squats, 8 push-ups, pigeon stretch, med ball shoulders. Work up to 60% of one rep maximum back squat. Then, 4 rounds: 8 back squat. Next: 80 double unders, (240 singles) 40 shoulder to overhead, 60 double unders, (180 singles) 30 shoulder to overhead, 40 double unders, (120 singles) 20 shoulder to overhead.

Home Edition:

- 3 minute jog around your block or jog in place
- 2 rounds: 8 air squats, 8 push-ups, 8 sit-ups
- 240 jumping jacks, 20 pike push-ups, 180 jumping jacks, 15 pike push-ups, 120 jumping jacks, 10 pike push-ups
- 5 minute max butterfly sit-ups

DAY 290

Original Session: Warm up - 400 meter run, 2 rounds: 10 air squat, 10 push-up, 10 kettlebell swing, dislocates. Then, 4 rounds: 10 dumbbell v-sit push press, 10/10 bent over row. Next, 800 meter run, then 6 rounds: 5 dumbbell deadlift, 5 dumbbell clean, 5 dumbbell thrusters. Finish with 800 meter run.

Home Edition:

- 1 minute jumping jacks, then 2 rounds: 10 air squats, 10 push-ups, 15 calf raises
- 4 rounds: 10 straight leg sit-ups, 10 diamond push-ups
- 40 burpees, then 6 rounds: 5 tuck jumps, 5 unweighted thrusters, 5 froggers. Finish with 40 burpees

DAY 291

Original Session: Warm up - 2 rounds: 200 meter run, then 5 each of: air squats, jump squats, pull-ups, push-ups, dislocates, instep stretch. Work to a heavy front squat. Then, 4 rounds of: 3 front squats, 100 meter sprint, walk back is rest. Finish with 3 rounds: 20 wall balls, 10 pull-ups, 20 overhead kettlebell swings, 10 pull-ups.

Home Edition:

- 2 rounds: 1 minute jog in place, 5 each of: air squats, jump squats, push-ups
- 4 rounds: 10 air squats, 10 burpees
- 3 rounds: 20 reverse lunges, 10 push-ups, 10 single leg raises each side

DAY 292

Original Session: Warm up - 5 minutes, 30 seconds moderate/30 seconds fast assault bike, then 2 rounds: 5/5 lunges, 5 box jumps, 10 push-ups, instep stretch, dislocates. Next, complete 5 rounds of: 10 dumbbell bench press, 10 push-ups, 1 rope climb. Finish with 6 rounds for time: 250 meter row.

Home Edition:

- 5 minute jog around your block or accumulate 5 minutes of: jog in place, stance jacks, high knees, calf raises, butt kickers
- 2 rounds: 5/5 reverse lunges, 5 air squats, 10 push-ups
- 5 rounds: 10 plank shoulder taps, 10 dive bomber push-ups
- 6 rounds: 10 pausing air squats, 10 single leg deadlift each leg

DAY 293

Original Session: Warm up - 2 rounds: 1 minute assault bike, 5 power cleans, 5 push presses, 5/5 lunges, pigeon stretch. 3 rounds: 8 power clean, up in weight each round, 400 meter run, 2 minute rest. Then, 3 rounds - 8 back squat, 30 seconds moderate/30 seconds fast assault bike x2, 90 seconds rest. Finish with 6 rounds of the following for time: 5 pull-ups, 10 push-ups, 15 air squats.

Home Edition:

- 2 rounds: 1 minute jog in place, 5 jump squats, 5 push-ups, 5/5 lunges
- 3 rounds: 16 stance jacks, 40 spiderman mountain climbers
- 3 rounds: 8 side planks with dip each side, 1 minute sprint in place
- 6 rounds: 5 push-ups, 10 plank shoulder taps, 15 air squats

DAY 294

Original Session: Warm up - 2 rounds: 200 meter run, 10 push-ups, 10 air squats, 5/5 lunges. Work to one rep max thruster. Then, 4 rounds: as many rounds as possible in 3 minutes of: 6 thrusters, 6 burpee box jumps, 1 minute rest between rounds.

Home Edition:

- 2 rounds: 25 jumping jacks, 10 push-ups, 10 air squats, 5/5 side lunges.
- 4 rounds, as many rounds as possible in 3 minutes: 6 froggers, 6 burpees
- Accumulate 5 minutes of a handstand hold

DAY 295

Original Session: Warm up - 2 rounds: 10/10 lunges, 5 dips, 5 push-ups, 5 box jumps, 5 pull-ups. Then, one partner works while the other partner holds a sandbag that cannot touch the ground. Switch as many times as needed to complete: 50 deadlifts, 50 toes to bar, 50 calorie row, 50 pull-ups, 50 box jumps.

Home Edition:

- 2 rounds: 10/10 lunges, 5 tricep dips, 5 push-ups, 5 air squats, 5 plank jacks
- 50 repetitions each: butterfly sit-ups, tuck jumps, flutter kicks, side step squats, (25 each side) scissor kicks, calf raises

DAY 296

MY DAD ENCOURAGED US TO FAIL. GROWING UP, HE WOULD ASK US WHAT WE FAILED AT THAT WEEK. IF WE DIDN'T HAVE SOMETHING, HE WOULD BE DISAPPOINTED. IT CHANGED MY MINDSET AT AN EARLY AGE THAT FAILURE IS NOT THE OUTCOME, FAILURE IS NOT TRYING. DON'T BE AFRAID TO FAIL. — SARA BLAKELY

Original Session: Warm up - 3 rounds: 30 second jump rope, 5 burpees, 5 dislocates, 30 second toe touches. 4 rounds: 10 z-press, 30 second rest, 5 box pike-up, 1 minute rest. As many rounds as possible in 14 minutes of: 7 muscle ups, 50 wall balls, 100 double unders (300 singles).

Home Edition:

- 3 rounds: 30 seconds jumping jacks, 5 burpees, 30 second calf raises
- 5 rounds: 20 floor switch kicks, 5 pike push-ups
- As many rounds as possible in 14 minutes of: 7 handstand push-ups, 50 air squats, 100 jumping jacks

DAY 297

Original Session: Warm up - 2 rounds: 1 minute assault bike, 5 front squats, 5 hang power cleans, 5 box jumps, sumo stretch. 5 rounds: 2 power cleans, 2 hang squat cleans, (up in weight each round) 90 second rest. Then, 5 rounds: 10 thrusters, 200 meter run, 90 second rest.

Home Edition:

- 2 rounds: 1 minute high knees, 5 air squats, 5/5 lunges, 5 jump squats
- 5 rounds: 3 wall walks, 10 unweighted thrusters
- 5 rounds: 15 burpees, 10 plank up downs
- 3 minute maximum butterfly sit-ups

DAY 298

Original Session: Warm up - 3 minute assault bike, then 2 rounds: 10 hollow rocks, 10 superman pedals, 10 push-ups, 10 goblet squats. 15 minute kipping technique practice. Then, 3 rounds for time: 400 meter run, 21 kettlebell swings, 12 pull-ups. Finish with 3 rounds: 10 ab roll outs.

Home Edition:

- 3 minute jog around your block or accumulate 3 minutes of: jog in place, mummy kicks, heisman
- 2 rounds: 10 hollow rocks, 10 superman pedals, 10 push-ups, 10 air squats
- Accumulate 5 minutes in a handstand hold or variation of your choice
- 3 rounds for time: 20 burpees, 21 pike push-ups, 12 twisting crunches
- 3 rounds: 1 minute plank hold

DAY 299

Original Session: Warm up - 400 meter run, then 2 rounds: 5/5 lunges, 10 air squat, 10 push-ups, instep stretch. 4 rounds: 10/10 Bulgarian split squat, 3/3 jump lunges. Fight gone bad: 3 rounds - 1 minute each station: sandbag over the shoulder, prowler push, man makers, burpee pull-ups, row or ski erg.

Home Edition:

- 3 minute jog around your block or jog in place
- 2 rounds: 5/5 lunges, 10 air squats, 10 push-ups
- 4 rounds: 10/10 reverse lunges, 3/3 jumping lunges
- 3 rounds, 1 minute each: frog jumps, wall walks, plank shoulder taps, unweighted man makers, v-up sit ups

DAY 300

Original Session: Warm up - 2 rounds: 1 minute assault bike, 5/5 lunges, 5 box jumps, 5 front squats, instep stretch. 10 minutes to work to a heavy front squat. Then at the top of each minute for 10 minutes, 2 front squats at 70% of maximum effort. Next, as many rounds as possible in 12 minutes of: 30 double unders, (90 singles) 20 kettlebell swings, 10 toes to bar.

Home Edition:

- 2 rounds: 1 minute high knees, 5/5 lunges, 5 jump squats, 5 push-ups
- At the top of each minute for 10 minutes: 5 single leg deadlift each side
- As many rounds as possible in 12 minutes of: 90 jumping jacks, 10 pike push-ups, 5 v-up sit-ups

DAY 301

Original Session: Warm up - 2 rounds: 200 meter run, 10 air squats, 10 push-ups, 10 box jumps, instep stretch. Then, 3 rounds: 8 ground to overhead, up in weight each round, 400 meter run, 2 minute rest. Next, 3 rounds: 8 deadlifts, 8 burpees, 1 minute assault bike. Finish with as many rounds as possible in 5 minutes of: 10/10 lunges, 10 weighted sit-ups, 10 slam balls.

Home Edition:

- 2 rounds: 1 minute each: jumping jacks, air squats, push-ups, one leg reach and jumps
- 3 rounds: 10 unweighted thrusters, 30 burpees
- 3 rounds: 8 inchworm to push-up, 8 lateral plank walks, 10 double leg raises
- As many rounds as possible in 5 minutes of: 10/10 lungess of choice, 10 Russian twist, 10 mountain climbers

DAY 302

Original Session: Warm up - 500 meter row, 2 rounds: 10 kettlebell swings, 10 goblet squats. Then, 5 rounds: 5 bench presses, up in weight each round, 5/5 kettlebell bent over row. Then, 5 rounds: 200 meter run, then as many rounds as possible against a 3 minute clock: 3 hang power cleans, 6 push-ups, 9 air squats.

Home Edition:

- 4 minute jog around your block or accumulate 4 minutes of: jog in place, jump rope side to side, mummy kicks, butt kickers
- 2 rounds: 10 push-ups, 10 sit-ups, 5 air squats
- 5 rounds: dive bomber push-ups, 30 second bear plank hold
- 5 rounds, as many rounds as possible against a 3 minute clock: 3 glute bridge walk outs, 6 floor switch kicks, 9 in and out abs

DAY 303

Original Session: Warm up - 2 rounds: 1 minute assault bike, 5 deadlifts, 5/5 lunges, 5 dumbbell push presses, sumo stretch. Work to a heavy deadlift. Then, 5 rounds: 3 deadlift at 85% of maximum effort, 3 box jumps, up in height each round. At the top of each minute for 20 minutes: 1 minute hard assault bike,

Home Edition:

- 2 rounds: 1 minute jog in place, 5 straight leg sit-ups, 5/5 lunges, 5 push-ups
- Accumulate 5 minutes in a wall sit hold
- 5 rounds: 5 glute bridge walk outs, 5 stance jacks
- At the top of each minute for 20 minutes: 4 plank up-downs, 10 flutter kicks, rest one minute

DAY 304

Original Session: Warm up - 2 rounds: 200 meter run, 5 back squat, 5/5 lunges, 5 pull-ups, 5 push-ups. With a partner: each completes all repetitions, one works at a time: 50 back squats, 500 meter row, 50 overhead kettlebell swing, 400 meter run, 50 hand release push-up, 500 meter row, 50 push press, 400 meter run.

Home Edition:

- 2 rounds: 25 jumping jacks, 5 air squats, 5/5 side lunges, 5 push-ups, 5 sit-ups
- 50 air squats, 50 overhead lunges, (25 each side) 50 hand release push-ups, 50 butterfly sit-ups

DAY 305

Original Session: Warm up - 400 meter run, then 3 rounds: 5 pull-ups, 10 push-ups, 15 air squats. 5 rounds: 6 dumbbell bench press, 6 pull-ups. Then, 3 rounds: 500 meter row, 6 muscle ups, 9 squat cleans. Finish with 3 rounds: 10/10 kettlebell thrasher, 45 second shoulder tap plank, 5 hanging leg raises

Home Edition:

- 50 jumping jacks, 15 sit-ups, 10 push-ups, 30 air squats
- 5 rounds: 2 wall walks
- 3 rounds: 20 burpees, 6 tuck jumps
- 3 rounds: 10/10 Russian twist, 30 seconds side plank each side, 5 double leg raises

DAY 306

Original Session: Warm up - 2 rounds: 30 second jump rope, 10/10 lunges, 5 deadlift, 10 push-ups, pigeon stretch. Work to a heavy deadlift. 5 round: 5 deadlifts, 100 meter sprint, walk back is rest. Until failure: Minute 1: 7 calorie row, 1 burpee. Minute 2: 7 calorie row, 2 burpees - continue until failure.

Home Edition:

- 2 rounds: 30 second jump rope in place, 10/10 lunges, 5 deadlifts, 10 push-ups
- 5 rounds: 5 v-up push-ups, 30 second sprint in place
- Until failure: minute 1: 2 burpees, minute 2: 4 burpees . . . add 2 burpees every minute until all burpees for the given time cannot be completed

DAY 307

Original Session: Warm up - 2 rounds: 200 meter run, 10 push press, 10 bent over row, med ball shoulders. Rope climb technique. Then, 5 rounds: 5 push presses, 1 rope climb. For time: 21 each: goblet squats, kettlebell swings, 200 meter run, 15 each: goblet squats, kettlebell swing, 200 meter run, 9 each: goblet squat, kettlebell swing, 200 meter run.

Home Edition:

- 2 rounds: 5 burpees, 10 mountain climbers, 20 high knees
- 5 rounds: 10 rope climb sit-ups
- 21 repetitions of: air squats, plank jacks, 1 minute sprint in place
- 15 repetitions of: squat jacks, in and out abs, 1 minute sprint in place
- 9 repetitions of: tuck jumps, plank up downs, 1 minute sprint in place

DAY 308

Original Session: Warm up - 400 meter run, then 2 rounds: 5/5 lunges, 10/10 banded side steps, 5 pull-ups, pigeon stretch. Then, 4 rounds: 6/6 sandbag lunges, 6/6 banded thrashers. Next, 3 rounds for time with a partner: Partner 1 completes 50 sandbag step ups while Partner 2 completes as many rounds possible of: 15 calorie row, 5 man makers, 5 toes to bar,

Home Edition:

- Jog around your block for 3 minutes or accumulate 3 minutes of: high knees, butt kickers, heisman
- 2 rounds: 5/5 lungess, 10 air squats, 5 push-ups
- 4 rounds: 12 forward to reverse lunges each side
- 50 lunges, then 5 rounds of: 5 unweighted man makers, 5 v-up sit-ups. Finish with 50 lunges

DAY 309

Original Session: Warm up - 5 minutes 30 seconds moderate/30 seconds fast assault bike, then 2 rounds: 5 pull-ups, 5 air squats, 10 kettlebell swings, dislocates, instep stretch, sumo stretch. In teams: 2,000 meter row, then 16 rounds: 4 heavy kettlebell swings, 8 push-ups, 12 sit-ups, 16 air squats. Finish with a 2,000 meter row.

Home Edition:

- 5 minutes: 30 seconds jog in place, 30 seconds calf raises
- 2 rounds: 5 push-ups, 10 air squats
- 50 burpees
- 8 rounds: 4 in and out abs, 8 push-ups, 12 sit-ups, 16 air squats
- 50 burpees

DAY 310

Original Session: Warm up - 2 rounds - 250 meter row, 5 front squats, 5 box jumps, 5/5 lunges, 5 push-ups. Work to a heavy front squat. Then, at the top of each minute for 8 minutes, perform 2 front squats, 2 strict pull-ups. Next, 3 rounds of: 15 ground to overhead unbroken (perform 20 wall balls if bar leaves hands).

Home Edition:

- 2 rounds: 30 seconds each: jog in place, pausing air squats, stance jacks, froggers, hand release push-ups
- 3 rounds: 1 minute wall sit hold
- At the top of each minute for 8 minutes: 2 side step squats each side, 4 lateral plank walks each side
- 3 rounds: 15 pike push-ups

DAY 311

Original Session: Warm up - At the top of each minute for 5 minutes: 5 push-ups, 5 air squats, 5 box jumps. Then, 5 rounds: 5 push press, up in weight each round, one heavy sled pull, 90 seconds rest. As many rounds as possible in 15 minutes of: 200 meter run, 20 overhead kettlebell swings, 20 air squats.

Home Edition:

- At the top of each minute for 5 minutes: 5 push-ups, 5 air squats, 5 jump squats
- 5 rounds: 5 diamond push-ups, 10 spiderman mountain climbers
- As many rounds as possible against a 15 minute clock of: 1 minute sprint in place, 20 air squats, 20 flutter kicks

DAY 312

Original Session: Warm up - 2 rounds: 200 meter run, 10 kettlebell swings, 10 air squats, 10 push-ups, instep stretch. Work to a heavy thruster. Next, 3 rounds: 500 meter row, 10 thrusters. Finish with 3 rounds: 10 Romanian deadlift with a heavy kettlebell.

Home Edition:

- 2 rounds: 1 minute jog in place, 10 jumping jacks, 10 air squats, 10 push-ups
- Accumulate 5 minutes in handstand or variation of choice
- 3 rounds: 20 burpees, 10 unweighted thrusters, 20 alternating front kicks
- 3 rounds: 20 alternating one leg Romanian deadlift

DAY 313

Original Session: Warm up - 3 rounds: 30 second jump rope, 5 military press, 5 push press, 5 front squat, 5/5 lunges. Work to a heavy push jerk. Then, 4 rounds: 6 shoulder to overhead, 6 bar over burpees, rest 3 minutes. 3 rounds: 10/10 front rack bar lunges, 200 meter run. Finish with deck of cards workout: push-ups, double unders, kettlebell swings, goblet squats, slam balls, toes to bar.

Home Edition:

- Deck of cards: Use the following movements and perform number of repetitions drawn of a given card:
- Hearts = diamond push-ups, spades = burpees, clubs = glute bridge walk outs, diamonds = air squats, jokers = 2 minute sprint in place. Aces = 1 minute plank hold, face cards = 10 repetitions each

DAY 314

Original Session: Warm up - 3 rounds, 30 seconds each: jump rope, lunges. 3 rounds: hang power cleans, then 3 rounds: 8/8 front rack lunges, 350 lunges. Finish with 2 rounds: 1 minute maximum effort assault bike.

Home Edition:

- 3 rounds, 30 seconds each: side to side jumps, lunges, push-ups, sit-ups
- 3 rounds: 10 pulsing side planks each side, 30 second hollow hold, 30 second superman hold
- 3 rounds: 20 side lunges each side
- 5 minute maximum tuck jumps

DAY 315

Original Session: Warm up - 1 minute assault bike, 10 ring rows, 10 pushups, 10 sit ups. 4 rounds: 10 dumbbell push press, 10 double kettlebell front squat. Then, as many rounds as possible in 10 minutes of: 5 deadlifts, 5 hang power cleans, 5 front squats, 5 push presses, 10 toes to bar.

Home Edition:

- 1 minute jog in place, 10 tricep dips, 10 push-ups, 10 sit-ups
- 4 rounds: 10 pike push-ups, 10 convict squats
- As many rounds as possible in 10 minutes of: 5 stance jacks, 5 froggers, 5 plank up downs, 5 in and out abs, 5 v-up sit-ups

DAY 316

Original Session: Warm up - 2 rounds: 1 minute jump rope, 5 burpees, dislocates, instep stretch, scarecrows. 4 rounds: 5 box drag pike-ups, 5/5 bent over rows. For time: 800 meter run, 40 wall balls, 400 meter run, 40 calorie assault bike, 200 meter run, 40 box jump overs.

Home Edition:

- 2 rounds; 1 minute jumping jacks, 5 burpees
- 4 rounds: 2 wall walks, 20 plank jacks
- 40 burpees, 40 air squats, 30 burpees, 30 mountain climbers, 20 burpees, 20 alternating jumping lunges

Day 317

Original Session: Warm up - 2 rounds: 5/5 lunges, 5 push-up, 5 air squat, 5 pull-ups, instep stretch. 3 rounds: 5 pull-ups, 10 push-ups, 15 air squats, 20 deadlifts, 200 meter run. 2 rounds: 5 pull-ups, 10 push-ups, 15 air squats, 15 squat cleans, 200 meter run. Finish with 5 pull-ups, 10 push-ups, 15 air squats, 10 power cleans, 200 meter run.

Home Edition:

- 2 rounds: 5/5 reverse lunges, 5 push-ups, 5 air squats, 5 straight leg sit ups
- 6 rounds: 5 pike push-ups, 10 mountain climbers, 15 air squats
- As many repetitions possible in 5 minutes of burpees

DAY 318

Original Session: Warm up - At the top of each minute for 5 minutes: 5 push-ups, 5 air squats, 1 gym length sprint. Next, 3 rounds: 8 thrusters, 4 burpees, 400 meter run, 90 seconds rest. Then, 3 rounds battle rope complex: 20/20 alternating, 20 slams, 20 jumping jacks, 20 slams.

Home Edition:

- At the top of each minute for 5 minutes: 5 push-ups, 5 air squats
- 200 burpees for time

DAY 319

Original Session: Warm up - 2 rounds, 10 repetitions each: back squat, push press, curls, instep stretch, dislocates. 5 rounds: 10 dumbbell curl to press, 10-15 tricep dips. Then, 3 rounds for time: 500 meter row, 10 back squats, 1 rope climb.

Home Edition:

- 2 rounds, 10 repetitions each: air squat, plank shoulder taps, spiderman mountain climbers
- 5 rounds: 10 plank up-downs, 15 tricep dips
- 3 rounds: 25 stance jacks, 10 air squats, one wall walk

DAY 320

Original Session: Warm up - 5 minutes: 30 seconds moderate/30 seconds fast assault bike. 5 rounds: 3 back squats, up in weight each round. Finish with 1,000 meter row, 50 thrusters, 30 pull-ups.

Home Edition:

- 5 minutes: 30 seconds high knees, 30 seconds calf raises
- 5 rounds: 1 minute wall sit hold, 30 seconds front kicks, 30 seconds side kicks left, 30 seconds side kicks right
- 5 minute run or 5 minute run in place, 50 unweighted man makers, 30 push-ups

DAY 321

Original Session: Warm up - 3 rounds line drills: lunges, high knees, butt kickers, then 10 Romanian deadlifts, 10 ball slams. Then, 3 rounds: 8 kettlebell Romanian deadlifts, 8 push presses, 60 seconds plank hold. Finish with 3 rounds: 400 meter row, 30 kettlebell swings, 30 air squats.

Home Edition:

- 3 rounds, 30 seconds each: lunges, high knees, butt kickers, heisman, mummy kicks, calf raises
- 3 rounds: 32 unweighted straight leg deadlifts, 8 inchworm to push-up, 1 minute plank hold
- 3 rounds: 20 froggers, 20 tuck jumps, 1 minute bear plank hold

DAY 322

Original Session: Warm up - 2 rounds: 30 second jump rope, 10 dislocates, 10 overhead squats, med ball shoulders, sumo stretch. Work to a heavy overhead squat. 3 rounds: 7 overhead squats, 21 wall balls, 7 ring rows, 7 dips. Finish with 3 rounds: 5 toe box drags, 20 second L-sit hold.

Home Edition:

- 1 minute jump rope in place, 10 convict squats, 5 push-ups
- 3 rounds: 15 convict squats, 20 reverse lunges each side, 10 floor switch kicks
- 3 rounds: 10 glute bridge walk outs, 30 second single leg glute bridge hold each side

DAY 323

Original Session: Warm up - 3 minute assault bike, then 2 rounds: 10 air squats, 10 kettlebell swings, 10 push-ups, dislocates, instep stretch. Then, 5 rounds: 3 back squat, up in weight each round. Next, as many rounds as possible in 12 minutes of: 6 toes to bar, 9 shoulder to overhead, 12 calorie assault bike. Finish with 4 rounds heavy prowler push.

Home Edition:

- 3 minute jog around your block or accumulate 3 minutes of: high knees, jumping jacks, heisman
- 2 rounds: 10 air squats, 10 butterfly sit-ups, 10 push-ups
- 5 rounds: 30 second wall sit, 30 second hollow hold
- As many rounds as possible in 12 minutes of: 6 v-up sit-ups, 9 pike push-ups, 12 burpees

DAY 324

Original Session: Warm up - 2 rounds: 200 meter run, 10 push press, 10 bent over row, pigeon stretch, med ball shoulders. Work to a heavy push press. Then, 4 rounds: 5 push press, 1 rope climb. For time: 100 calorie row, every 2 minutes, stop and complete 25 wall balls, until 100 calories are complete.

Home Edition:

- 2 rounds: 1 minute jog in place, 10 push-ups, 10 air squats
- Accumulate 5 minutes in a handstand hold
- 4 rounds: 5 wide grip push-ups, 5 rope climb sit-ups
- 50 burpees (every 2 minutes stop and complete 10 tricep dips, until burpees are complete)

DAY 325

Original Session: Warm up - 2 rounds: 5 deadlift, 5/5 lunges, 5 box jump, 5 pull-ups, sumo stretch. Work to a heavy deadlift. Then, 4 rounds: 12 deadlifts at 75% bodyweight, 12 pull-ups, 200 meter run. For time: 100 butterfly sit-ups.

Home Edition:

- 2 rounds: 5 unweighted thrusters, 5/5 lunges, 5 jump squats, 10 in and out abs
- 4 rounds: 10 marching glute bridges, 10 spiderman mountain climbers, 10 unweighted man makers, 10 single leg reach and jump each leg
- 100 butterfly sit-ups

DAY 326

Original Session: Warm up - 5 minutes: 30 seconds moderate/30 seconds fast assault bike. 3 rounds: 20 kettlebell swings, 10 push-ups, 500 meter row, 2 minute rest. 3 rounds: 20 goblet squats, 5 box jumps, 30 seconds moderate/30 seconds fast assault bike x2, 90 seconds rest. For time: 75 slam balls or wall balls.

Home Edition:

- 5 minutes, 30 seconds each: jumping jacks, side to side lunges
- 3 rounds: 20 ski down abs, 10 plank shoulder taps, 1 minute sprint in place
- 3 rounds: 20 air squats, 5 jump squats, 1 minute sprint in place
- 75 glute bridge raises

DAY 327

Original Session: Warm up - 2 rounds: 5 front squat, 5 hang squat clean, 5 push press, 5 push-ups, sumo stretch. Work to a heavy clean and jerk. At the top of each minute for 8 minutes: 1 squat clean, 1 squat clean & jerk. Finish with 4 rounds: 25 calorie assault bike, 300 meter row, 400 meter run.

Home Edition:

- 2 rounds: 5 air squat, 5 push-up, 10 straight leg sit ups
- At the top of each minute for 8 minutes, 8 jump squats, 8 forward and back lunges each side
- 4 rounds: 20 burpees, 20 ski down abs, 10 single leg raises each side

DAY 328

Original Session: Warm up - 3 minute row, 2 rounds: 10 push-up, 5 scarecrow, instep stretch, dislocates. Then, 2 rounds: 10/10, 8/8, 6/6 repetitions of: bench press, dumbbell row. For time: 500 meter ski erg, 50 calorie airdyne, 800 meter row.

Home Edition:

- 5 minute jog around your block or accumulate 5 minutes of: jog in place, jump rope in place, mummy kicks, high knees, heisman
- 2 rounds: 10/10, 8/8, 6/6 repetitions of: side plank dips, plank up-downs, single arm glute bridge pulses
- 50 burpees, 25 lunges each side, 20 floor switch kicks

DAY 329

Original Session: Warm up - 2 rounds: 200 meter run, 5 inch worms, 5 pull-ups, 5/5 lunges, 5/5 side lunges, instep stretch, dislocates. Then, 5 rounds: 30 second handstand hold, 30 second hollow hold, 30 second rest. Finish with partner med ball hold: one partner doesn't let the med ball touch the ground while the other works, switch as needed: 200 meter run, 60 wall balls, 200 meter run, 40 pull-ups, 200 meter run, 30 burpees, 200 meter run, 40 pull-ups, 200 meter run, 60 wall balls, 200 meter run.

Home Edition:

- 2 rounds: 1 minute jumping jacks, 5 inch worm walk outs, 5/5 reverse lunges, 5/5 side step squat
- 5 rounds: 30 second handstand hold, 30 seconds hollow hold, 30 seconds superman hold
- 1 minute sprint, 30 air squats, 1 minute sprint, 20 push-ups, 1 minute sprint, 15 burpees, 1 minute sprint, 20 plank up-downs, 1 minute sprint, 60 alternating lunges, 1 minute sprint

DAY 330

Original Session: Warm up - 2 rounds: 30 second jump rope, 3 wall walks, 5 push-ups, dislocates. 5 rounds, 3 bench press, up in weight each round, 3 strict pull-ups. Then, 4 rounds against a 2 minute clock: 200 meter run, then as many rounds as possible of: burpee box jumps, rest one minute between rounds

Home Edition:

- 2 rounds, 30 second jumping jacks, 1 minute wall sit hold, 5 push-ups, 5 sit-ups
- 5 rounds: 6 pike push-ups with hold at the bottom, 10 double leg raises
- 4 rounds against a 2 minute clock: 30 high knees, fill remaining time with as many burpees as possible

DAY 331

Original Session: Warm up - 2 rounds: 1 minute assault bike, 5/5 lunges, 10 push press, instep stretch. At the top of each minute for 20 minutes: odd numbers = 8 deadlifts, up in weight each round, even numbers = 5 toes to bar. For time: 50 repetitions each: double unders, (150 singles) box jump overs, calorie row, double unders (150 singles).

Home Edition:

- 2 rounds: 1 minute slow side to side lunges, 10 push-ups, 5/5 quad stretch
- At the top of each minute for 20 minutes: odd numbers = 8 burpees, even numbers = 20 scissor kicks
- 50 repetitions each: jumping jacks, jump squats, stance jacks

DAY 332

Original Session: Warm up - 400 meter run, 2 rounds: 10 air squat, 5/5 scarecrow, 10 ring rows, pigeon stretch. 4 rounds: 12 v-sit press, 6/6 bent over row (5 seconds up/5 seconds down). For time: 800 meter run, 75 ground to overhead, 800 meter run. 3 rounds: 5 toe box drag.

Home Edition:

- 3 minute jog around your block or jog in place
- 2 rounds: 10 air squats, 5 inch worm walk outs, 10 tricep dips
- 4 rounds, 10 single leg glute bridge pulses each side, 12 plank up-downs
- 30 burpees, 75 unweighted thrusters, 30 burpees
- 3 rounds: 5 v-up-sit ups

DAY 333

Original Session: Warm up - 5 push-ups, 10 air squats, 5 box jumps, dislocates, instep stretch, pigeon stretch. Work to a heavy hang squat clean. Then, 4 rounds: 3 hang squat cleans. Next, 4 rounds: 400 meter run, 1 rope climb, 10 heavy sandbag over the shoulder, 10 scotty Bobs.

Home Edition:

- 5 push-ups, 10 air squats, 5 jumping lunges each side
- 3 rounds: 1 minute wall sit, 30 seconds hollow hold, 30 seconds superman hold
- 4 rounds: 10/10 side squat lunges
- 4 rounds: 20 froggers, 1 wall walk, 10 unweighte scotty Bobs

DAY 334

Original Session: Warm up - 3 minute assault bike, 5/5 lunges, 10 push-up, 10 air squat, instep stretch. 4 rounds: 5/5 weighted step ups, 30 second assault bike sprint. At the top of each minute for as long as possible, burpee pull-ups until failure (start with 4, add 2 each round).

Home Edition:

- 3 minute jog around your block or jog in place, 5/5 reverse lunges, 10 push-ups, 10 air squats.
- 4 rounds: 10/10 jumping lunges, 30 second sprint in place
- At the top of each minute for as long as possible, burpees until failure. Start with 4, add 2 each minute, until unable to complete all repetitions within the minute

DAY 335

Original Session: Warm up - 400 meter run, 2 rounds: 5 pull-ups, 10 push-ups, 15 air squats. Then, 3 rounds: 8 deadlift, up in weight each round, 4 box jumps, 400 meter run, rest 2 minutes. Next, 3 rounds: 10/10 kettlebell snatch or 20 heavy kettlebell swings, 2 minute row (30 second moderate/30 second fast x2). Finish with 3 rounds battle rope complex - 20 slams, 20/20 side to side, 20/20 alternate, 20 jumping jacks.

Home Edition:

- 5 minute jog around your block, or accumulate 5 minutes of: jog in place, jumping jacks, mummy kicks, heisman, high knees
- 2 rounds: 10 plank shoulder taps, 15 air squats, 20 sit-ups
- 3 rounds: 20 alternating front kicks, 20 alternating side kicks, 20 alternating reverse lunges, 10 tuck jumps
- 1 minute each: flutter kicks, side plank pulses right, side plank pulses left, rope climb sit-ups, bicycle crunches

DAY 336

Original Session: Warm up - 2 rounds: 200 meter run, 10 air squats, 10 kettlebell swings, 10 push-ups, sumo stretch. 5 rounds: 10 curl to press, 5 push-ups or strict pull-ups, 2 minute rest. Finish with as many rounds as possible in 20 minutes of: 15 calorie row, 9 wall balls.

Home Edition:

- 2 rounds: 30 second jog in place, 10 air squats, 10 push-ups
- 5 rounds: 20 floor switch kicks, 20 in and out abs
- As many rounds as possible in 20 minutes of: 10 burpees, 5 air squats

DAY 337

Original Session: Warm up - 2 rounds: 1 minute assault bike, 5 squat cleans, 5 box jumps, 5/5 lunges. Work to a heavy squat clean. Then, at the top of each minute for 6 minutes: 2 squat cleans. For time: 15 toes to bar, 20 bar over burpees, 30 thrusters, 20 bar over burpees, 15 toes to bar.

Home Edition:

- 2 rounds, one minute each: stance jacks, jumping lunges, pausing air squats
- At the top of each minute for 6 minutes: 10 unweighted renegade rows
- 15 v-up sit-ups, 20 burpees, 30 unweighted thrusters, 20 burpees, 15 v-up sit-ups

DAY 338

Original Session: Warm up - 1 minute assault bike, 5/5 lunges. Partner 1: 200 meter run, while partner 2 does wall balls wall balls while partner 2 runs 200 meters, 3 rope climbs together, ground to overheads while partner 2 runs 200 meters, run 200 meter while partner 2 does ground to overheads, 1 rope climb together. Finish with 2,500 meter row for time.

Home Edition:

- 50-40-30-20-10 repetitions of: burpees, butterfly sit-ups, jumping jacks

DAY 339

Original Session: Warm up - 5 minutes, 30 seconds moderate/30 seconds fast assault bike, dislocates, scarecrow. 5 rounds: 10 v-press right, 10 bent over row right, 10 v-press left, 10 bent over row left. At the top of each minute for 20 minutes: even numbers = 12 calorie row, odd numbers = 5 box jumps, 5 dumbbell thrusters

Home Edition:

- 5 minutes: 30 seconds mountain climbers, 30 seconds slow burpees
- 5 rounds: 10 pike push-ups, 10 glute bridge walk outs, 10 standing oblique crunches each side
- At the top of each minute for 20 minutes: even numbers = sprint in place, odd numbers = froggers

DAY 340

Original Session: Warm up - 2 rounds: 1 minute assault bike, 5 burpees, instep stretch, dislocates. Then, 3 rounds: 10 shoulder to overhead, 90 seconds row, 90 seconds rest. 3 rounds: 10/10 walking lunges, 400 meter run, 90 seconds rest. Finish with 30 burpee pull-ups for time.

Home Edition:

- 2 rounds: 1 minute jog in place, 5 burpees, 5 inchworm walkouts
- 3 rounds: max handstand hold
- 3 rounds: 10/10 walking lunges, 20 burpees
- 100 butterfly sit-ups for time

DAY 341

Original Session: Warm up - 2 rounds: 250 meter row, 5/5 lunges, 5 scarecrows, dislocates. Handstand technique, followed by 3 rounds: 5-10 handstand push-ups, 5-10 strict pull-ups. For time: 21-15-9 repetitions of: burpee box jumps, assault bike calories (42-30-18)

Home Edition:

- 2 rounds: 5/5 lunges, 10 butt kickers, 10 marching toe touches, 5 push-ups
- 3 rounds: 5-10 handstand push-ups or handstand hold
- 21-15-9 repetitions of: burpees, single leg deadlift each side, plank jacks, scissor kicks

DAY 342

Original Session: Warm up - 2 rounds: 5 air squats, 5/5 lunges, 10 push-ups, dislocates, instep stretch. 4 rounds: 10 kettlebell front squat, 10/10 barbell twist. 3 rounds: 40/30 calorie row, ball slams, box jumps, gym length sprint, bench press.

Home Edition:

- 2 rounds: 5 air squats, 5/5 lunges, 10 push-ups, 30 second jog in place or jumping jacks
- 4 rounds: 10 air squats, 10 side step lunges each side, 20 Russian twists
- 10-20-30-40-50 repetitions of: plank jacks, high knees, plank shoulder taps, calf raises, glute bridge pulses

DAY 343

Original Session: Warm up - 2 rounds: 5 hang power cleans, 10 air squats, 5 box jumps, 10 push-ups, instep stretch, sumo stretch. Work to a heavy power clean, then at the top of each minute for 8 minutes, complete 2 power cleans at 70-80% of maximum effort. Finish with 200 kettlebell swings (at the top of each minute, sop and do 5 burpees until swings are complete).

Home Edition:

- 2 rounds: 5 stance jacks, 10 air squats, 5 jump squats, 10 push-ups.
- At the top of each minute for 8 minutes: 8 air squats, 4 plyo push-ups
- 200 jumping jacks (at the top of each minute stop and complete 5 v-up sit-ups)

DAY 344

Original Session: Warm up - 2 rounds: 10 air squats, 10 push-ups, 10 box jumps, sumo stretch, dislocates. 10-9-8-7-6-5-4-3-2-1 repetitions of bench press, up in weight, against a running clock. As many rounds as possible in 5 minutes: 1) 21 calorie assault bike, 21 deadlifts. 2) 15 calorie assault bike, 15 front squat. 3) 9 calorie assault bike, 9 thrusters.

Home Edition:

- 2 rounds: 10 air squats, 10 push-ups, 10 jumping lunges each side
- 10-9-8-7-6-5-4-3-2-1 repetitions of: wide grip push-ups, glute bridge
- As many rounds as possible in 5 minutes of: 21 burpees, 21 butterfly sit-ups
- As many rounds as possible in 5 minutes of: 15 froggers, 15 sumo stance squats
- As many rounds as possible in 5 minutes of: 9 plank up-downs, 9 in and out abs

DAY 345

Original Session: Warm up - 2 rounds, 5 repetitions each: front squat, push press, box jump, push-up. Then, work to a heavy clean & jerk. Next, 5 rounds: 1 clean & jerk at 80% of maximum effort. For time: 800 meter run, then 3 rounds: 30 double unders (90 singles) 20 wall balls, 10 burpee box jumps. Finish with an 800 meter row.

Home Edition:

- 2 rounds: 5 air squat, 5 push-up, 10 spiderman mountain climbers
- 5 rounds: 10 tricep dips, 30 second hollow hold, 30 second superman hold, 20 standing oblique crunches each side
- 30 burpees, 30 stance jacks, 30 ski abs, 30 reverse lunges

DAY 346

Original Session: Warm up - 3 rounds: gym length of the following: lunges, high knees, butt kickers. Then 10 good mornings, 10 ball slams. 3 rounds: 8 single leg deadlift, 1 minute rest, 10 dumbbell push press, 1 minute rest. As many rounds as possible in 15 minutes of: 30 double unders, (90 singles) 3 sandbag over shoulder, 30 box jumps, 2 rope climbs, 15 weighted sit-ups, 2 wall walks.

Home Edition:

- 1 minute each: High knees, butt kickers, side lunges, reverse lunges, straight leg sit-ups
- 3 rounds, 8/8 single leg deadlifts, 8/8 side plank pulses
- Twisting crunch ladder: Sit up - 10 twists, sit up - 8 twists, 6, 4, 2. Repeat 3 times
- As many rounds as possible in 15 minutes: 90 jumping jacks, 30 air squats, 5 double leg raises, 2 wall walks

DAY 347

Original Session: Warm up - 2 rounds: 1 minute assault bike, 5/5 lunges, 10 push-up, instep stretch, dislocates. 5 rounds: 5 deadlifts, up in weight each round, 5 box jumps. For time: 4 rounds: 5 pull-ups, 10 push-ups, 15 air squats, then 9 ground to overhead. 4 rounds: 5 pull-ups, 10 push-ups, 15 air squats, then 7 ground to overhead. 4 rounds: 5 pull-ups, 10 push-ups, 15 air squats, then 5 ground to overhead.

Home Edition:

- 2 rounds: 1 minute each: jog in place, reverse lunges, push-ups
- 5 rounds: 5 slow pike push-ups, 5 jump squats
- 4 rounds: 5 v-up sit-ups, 10 push-ups, 15 air squats, then 1 minute bear plank hold.
- 4 rounds: 5 v-up sit-ups, 10 push-ups, 15 air squats, then 2 minutes floor switch kicks

DAY 348

Original Session: Warm up - 500 meter row, 2 rounds: 5 ring rows, 5/5 lunges, 10 push-up, instep stretch, dislocates. 3 rounds: 8 power cleans, 45 second assault bike sprint, 90 second rest. Then, 3 rounds: 12 front rack lunges, 200 meter run, 90 second rest. Finish with 3 rounds: 10 dumbbell curl to press, 10 bent over fly, 60 second plank shoulder taps, 10/10 Russian twist.

Home Edition:

- 4 minute jog around your block or jog in place, 2 rounds: 5 tricep dips, 5/5 reverse lunges, 10 diamond push-ups
- 3 rounds: 8 tuck jumps, 45 second sprint in place
- 3 rounds: 6/6 jumping lunges, 20 spiderman mountain climbers
- 3 rounds: 30 second plank hold, 30 second elevated side plank right, 30 second elevated side plank left

DAY 349

Original Session: Warm up - At the top of each minute for 5 minutes: 5 box jumps, 5 air squats, 5 push-ups. With a partner: 400 meter run, then 5 rounds: 5 hang power clean, 10 push-up, 15 air squat. 400 meter run, then: 5 rounds: 5 deadlift, 10 box jump, 15 wall balls, 400 meter run.

Home Edition:

- At the top of each minute for 5 minutes: 5 box jumps, 5 air squats, 5 push-ups
- 20 burpees, then 5 rounds:5 tuck jumps, 10 push-ups, 15 air squats
- 20 burpees, then 5 rounds: 5 v-up sit-ups, 10 jump squats, 15 jumping jacks, 20 burpees

DAY 350

Original Session: Warm up - at the top of each minute for 5 minutes: 5 push-ups, 5 air squats, down and back gym sprints. 5 rounds: 5-10 strict pull-ups, 10 dumbbell bench presses. Then, 3 rounds: 50 air squat, 40 double unders, (120 singles) 30 overhead kettlebell swings. Finish with accumulating 5 minutes of heavy farmer carry.

Home Edition:

- At the top of each minute for 5 minutes: 5 push-ups, 5 air squats, 5 jumping jacks
- 5 rounds: 5 hand release push-ups
- 3 rounds: 50 air squats, 40 plank jacks, 30 overhead lunges
- 20 inch worm walk outs, 10 single leg raises, 20 standing oblique crunches each side

DAY 351

Original Session: Warm up - 10 repetitions each: kettlebell swings, box jumps, push-ups, 10/10 lunges. Work to a heavy back squat. Then, 5 rounds: 3 back squats, 30 second row sprint. Finish with as many rounds as possible in 12 minutes of: 5/5 kettlebell snatch, 10 toes to bar, 10 burpee box jumps.

Home Edition:

- 10 repetitions each: v-up sit-ups, jump squats, push-ups, 10/10 reverse lunges.
- 3 rounds: 1 minute wall sit
- 5 rounds: 3 wall walks, 30 second sprint in place
- As many rounds as possible in 12 minutes of: 10 convict squats, 10 double leg raises, 10 burpees

DAY 352

Original Session: Warm up - 2 rounds: 250 meter row, 5 deadlifts, 5/5 lunge, 5 push-ups, pigeon stretch. Work to a heavy deadlift. Then, 5 rounds: 3 deadlifts, 1 heavy prowler push, rest as needed. Next, 50-40-30-20-10 repetitions of: butterfly sit-ups, double unders (triple the amount for singles).

Home Edition:

- 2 rounds: 1 minute jog in place, 5 sit-ups, 5/5 lunges, 5 push-ups
- Accumulate 5 minutes in plank hold of choice
- 50-40-30-20-10 repetitions of: butterfly sit ups, burpees

DAY 353

Original Session: Warm up - 2 rounds: 200 meter run, 5 pull-ups, 5/5 lunges, 5 power cleans, instep stretch. With a partner: 1,500 meter row, 40 burpees, 30 wall balls, 20 power cleans, 1,000 meter row, 30 burpees, 20 wall balls, 10 power cleans, 500 meter row, 20 burpees, 10 wall balls, 5 power cleans.

Home Edition:

- 2 rounds: 1 minute high knees, 5 push-ups, 5/5 reverse lunges, 5 sit-ups
- 3 minute jumping jacks, then: 40 burpees, 30 air squats, 20 tuck jumps
- 2 minute stance jacks, then: 30 burpees 20 air squats, 10 tuck jumps

DAY 354

> *IF YOU HAVE STRENGTH OF CHARACTER, YOU CAN USE THAT AS FUEL TO NOT ONLY BE A SURVIVOR BUT TO TRANSCEND SIMPLY BEING A SURVIVOR, USE AN INTERNAL ALCHEMY TO TURN SOMETHING ROTTEN AND HORRIBLE INTO GOLD.*
> *— ZEENA SCHRECK*

Original Session: Warm up - 400 meter run, 2 rounds: 10 push-ups, 5 inch worms, 10/10 lunges, instep stretch, pigeon stretch. 5 rounds: 30 second handstand hold, 30 seconds rest, 30 seconds hollow hold, 30 seconds rest. For time: 1,000 meter row, 100 double unders, (300 singles) 30 dumbbell clusters, 500 meter row, 50 double unders, (150 singles) 20 dumbbell clusters, 250 meter row, 25 double unders, (75 singles) 10 dumbbell clusters.

Home Edition:

- 4 minute jog around your block or accumulate 4 minutes of: high knees, butt kickers, toe touches, lunge and twist over front leg
- 5 rounds: 30 second handstand hold, 30 second rest, 30 second hollow hold, 30 second rest
- For time: 3 minute sprint in place, 100 jumping jacks, 30 plank jacks, 2 minute sprint in place, 75 jumping jacks, 20 ski down abs, 1 minute sprint in place, 50 jumping jacks, 10 in and out abs

DAY 355

Original Session: Warm up - 2 rounds: 1 minute assault bike, 5/5 lunge, 5 overhead squat, 5 pull-ups, dislocates. Overhead squat technique, work to a heavy single. As many rounds as possible in 12 minutes of: 5 toes to bar, 10 burpee box jumps, 15 wall balls. Kipping technique.

Home Edition:

- 2 rounds: 1 minute butt kickers or high knees, 5/5 lunges, 5 convict squats, 5 push-ups.
- 5 rounds: 10 convict squats
- As many rounds as possible in 12 minutes of: 5 v-up sit-ups, 5 double leg raises, 10 burpees, 15 air squats

DAY 356

Original Session: Warm up - 2 rounds: 1 minute assault bike, 10 push-ups, 10 air squats, 5 jump squats. 3 rounds: 10 barbell jump squats, 1 minute row sprint, 90 seconds rest. Then, 3 rounds: 12 kettlebell deadlifts, 200 meter sprint, 90 seconds rest. Finally, 3 rounds: 10 Arnold press, 5 pull-ups, 10 GHD hip extensions.

Home Edition:

- 2 rounds: 1 minute mountain climbers, 10 push-ups, 10 air squats, 5 jump squats.
- 3 rounds: 10 jumping lunges, one minute burpees
- 3 rounds: 12 flutter kicks, 2 minutes burpees
- 3 rounds: 10 pike push-ups, 1 minute superman hold

DAY 357

Original Session: Warm up - 2 rounds: 250 meter row, 8 push-ups, 1 wall walk, dislocates, sumo. 4 rounds: 5 toe box drag, 5 toes to bar, 90 second rest. 3 rounds: 400 meter run, 21 burpees, 500 meter row.

Home Edition:

- 2 rounds: 20 jumping jacks, 8 push-ups, 1 wall walk
- 4 rounds: 2 wall walks, 8 double leg raises
- 3 rounds: 20 burpees, 20 standing oblique crunches each side, 20 spiderman mountain climbers

DAY 358

Original Session: Warm up - 2 rounds: 30 second jump rope, 5/5 lunge, 5 air squat, 5 front squat. 4 rounds: 4 front squat, up in weight each round, 4 box jumps. For time: 12-10-8-6-4-2 repetitions of: front rack lunges, pull-ups. Finish with 50 slam balls.

Home Edition:

- 2 rounds: 30 second jump in place, 5/5 lunge, 5 air squat, 5 front squat
- 4 rounds: 8 pausing air squats, 4 jump squats
- 12-10-8-6-4-2 repetitions of: reverse lunges, push-ups
- 50 burpees for time

DAY 359

Original Session: Warm up - 400 meter run, then 2 rounds: 10/10 banded lateral walks, 10 push-ups, 5/5 lunges, dislocates, instep stretch. 4 rounds: 10/10 kettlebell snatch, 10/10 Z press. 3 rounds: partner 1 rows 250 meters while partner 2 stands in double kettlebell front rack hold. 2 rounds: 10/10 single leg glute bridge pulses, 10 good mornings.

Home Edition:

- 3 minute jog around your block or jog in place, 2 rounds: 10/10 squat side steps, 10 push-ups, 5/5 lunges
- 4 rounds: 10 side plank with elbow floor taps each side, 20 in and out abs
- 3 rounds: max handstand hold
- 2 rounds: 10/10 single glute bridge pulses, 10 unweighted good mornings

DAY 360

Original Session: Warm up - 2 rounds: 5 tricep dips, 10 air squats, 15 sit-ups, 10/10 lunges, 200 meter run. 400 meter run, then: 25 kettlebell swings, 2 gym length heavy farmers carry, 2 lengths waiter carry, 2 lengths lunges, 25 box jumps, 200 meter run, 25 burpees, 400 meter sandbag run, 70 ball slams. Finish with 10 minute prowler relay.

Home Edition:

- Pick your poison:
- 300 burpees
- 2 mile run
- 100 air squats, 100 mountain climbers, 100 jumping jacks

DAY 361

Original Session: Warm up - 10 kettlebell swings, 10/10 lunges, 10 box jumps, sumo, instep stretch. Work to a heavy clean & jerk. Then at the top of each minute for 7 minutes: 1 clean & jerk. Next, 6 rounds: 250 meter row sprint. Finish with 200' heavy kettlebell farmer carry.

Home Edition:

- 10 v-up sit-ups, 10/10 reverse lunges, 10 jump squats
- At the top of each minute for 7 minutes, 10 tuck jumps
- 6 rounds: 30 floor switch kicks, 5 glute bridge walk outs
- Max handstand hold

DAY 362

Original Session: Warm up - 5 minutes: 30 seconds moderate/30 seconds fast assault bike. Then, 3 rounds: 8 hang power cleans, 15 air squats, 250 meter row, rest 90 seconds. Next, 3 rounds: 8 thrusters, 8 pull-ups, 2 minute assault bike, rest 90 seconds. Finish with 3 rounds battle rope complex: 20 slams, 20/20 wave, 20 jumping jacks.

Home Edition:

- 5 minutes: 30 seconds jog in place/30 seconds calf raises
- 3 rounds: 20 tuck jumps, 15 side step lunges each side
- 3 rounds: 20 unweighted thrusters, 8 hand release push-ups
- 100 butterfly sit-ups for time

DAY 363

All that is gold does not glitter, Not all those who wander are lost; The old that is strong does not wither, Deep roots are not reached by the frost. From the ashes a fire shall be woken, A light from the shadows shall spring; Renewed shall be the blade that was broken, The crownless again shall be king. —J.R.R. Tolkien

Original Session: Warm up - 500 meter row, 2 rounds: 5 box jumps, 10 kettlebell swings, 10 air squat, pigeon stretch, dislocates. Work to a heavy deadlift. Then, 5 rounds: 5 deadlifts, 10 push-ups, 90 seconds rest. For time: 400 meter run, 15 ground to overhead, 15 weighted sit-ups, 400 meter run, 10 ground to overhead, 10 weighted sit-ups, 400 meter run, 5 ground to overhead, 5 weighted sit-ups.

Home Edition:

- 3 minute jog in place, 2 rounds: 5 jump squats, 10 inch worm walk outs, 10 air squats
- 5 rounds: 5 wall walks, 10 push-ups
- 40 burpees, 15 convict squats, 15 straight leg sit ups, 40 burpees, 10 in and out abs, 10 flutter kicks, 40 burpees, 5 hollow rocks, 5 double leg raises

DAY 364

Original Session: Warm up - At the top of each minute for 5 minutes: 3 burpees, 4 down and back gym sprints. 5 rounds: 10 curl to press, 5-10 pull-ups. Then, as many rounds as possible in 5 minutes of: 10 hang power clean, 10 toes to bar, 90 seconds rest. Then, as many rounds as possible in 4 minutes of: 10 overhead kettlebell swings, 10 wall balls, 1 minute rest. Finally, many rounds as possible in 3 minutes of: 10 dumbbell thruster, 10 burpee box jumps.

Home Edition:

- At the top of each minute for 5 minutes: 3 burpees, 20 second sprint in place
- 5 rounds: 10 diamond push-ups, 10 marching glute bridges
- As many rounds as possible in 5 minutes of: 10 tuck jumps, 10 v-up-sit ups, as many rounds as possible in 4 minutes of: 10 spiderman mountain climbers, 10 air squats, as many rounds as possible in 3 minutes of: 10 renegade rows, 10 straight leg sit-ups

DAY 365

EVERY MAN'S HEART ONE DAY BEATS ITS FINAL BEAT. HIS LUNGS BREATHE THEIR FINAL BREATH. AND IF WHAT THAT MAN DID IN HIS LIFE MAKES THE BLOOD PULSE THROUGH THE BODY OF OTHERS AND MAKES THEM BELIEVE DEEPER IN SOMETHING THAT'S LARGER THAN LIFE, THEN HIS ESSENCE, HIS SPIRIT, WILL BE IMMORTALIZED BY THE STORYTELLERS - BY THE LOYALTY, BY THE MEMORY OF THOSE WHO HONOR HIM, AND MAKE THE RUNNING THE MAN DID LIVE FOREVER.
— JAMES BRIAN HELLWIG

Original Session: Warm up - 2 rounds: 200 meter run, 10 air squats, 5 box jumps, 10 kettlebell swings, dislocates. With a partner, hold a sandbag while the other partner works. 3 rounds: 1,000 meter run, 42 box jumps, 24 bodyweight deadlifts. Finish with 3 rounds battle rope complex: 20 slams, 20/20 alternate, 20/20 twist, 20 jumping jacks.

Home Edition:

- 2 rounds: 1 minute sprint in place, 10 air squats, 5 jump squats, 10 push-ups
- 3 rounds: 50 burpees, 42 jump squats, 24 push-ups
- 3 rounds: 20 Russian twists, 20 standing oblique crunches each side, 20 flutter kicks

COMMON CONCERNS AND COMMON SENSE ADVICE

It is understood that there are many concerns and reservations folks may have when considering whether or not this kind of training is right for them, especially when they get a few weeks into it and begin to have questions. I've included the following as my take on some of the things I've been asked throughout my journey just in case you may have wondered the same. Feel free to dig further if you'd like!

WILL I GET SORE? YES, EXPECT SORENESS. A LOT OF IT

Yes, you can expect to be sore if you haven't done anything like this in a while. You will soon be made keenly aware of muscles and connective tissue you didn't know existed, and sitting back into a chair or onto the toilet will be a historic journey altogether.

My advice is to pound the fish oil capsules, get a good magnesium supplement, as well as a good source of several types of collagen (the powder with 5 different sources of collagen is best). All of these things eat away at inflammation and will help you to bounce back faster. Another piece of advice on soreness: do not stay stagnant. The common recommendation for someone just starting out is to try and get their training in 2-3 days a week tops, with breaks in between workouts anywhere from 2-3 days. For those just starting out, do not try and blow through this book quickly. Instead, plan your rest days accordingly. This helps ensure that a beginner does not get burnt out or injured, by giving the body time to bounce back. This does not however, mean one should go into full on rest mode on your days off.

Instead, on your off days it will help immensely to go on a few short, easy walks throughout the day to keep things moving. If you cannot get out into the fresh air, make it a point to stand up every half hour or so and take a walk around the office. Do a set of 5 air squats every time you have to use the restroom, or a few toe to overhead reaches. Although it may be painful to move around, sitting still will make soreness worse. Don't forget to move.

WHAT IF I GET HURT?

Yep, injuries have the potential to happen no matter what kind of physical activity is being performed. An unconditioned person can snap an achilles tendon while taking off after their dog down the street, or throw their back out when picking up a small child.

The two questions that come to mind are: Are you content with risking an injury due to inactivity, or would you rather try easing into functional movement in a controlled, safe setting, to avoid such an injury in the first place? As with anything, the key here is to let the body ease its way into the work slowly. Bones, muscles, and connective tissue all have a lot of new things to learn, so it is ideal if these things can be done slowly and carefully.

On the flip side, if you suddenly have to jump out of the way of a car, you won't have the luxury of easing into any of that slowly. You're going to load your leg muscles, joints, tendons, and tissues, and hope that your springs don't snap upon take off or landing. In your home training sessions however, you can use the combination of your level of comfortability with a movement, along with what you feel you can handle next, to safely guide the body to become strong in a vast variety of everyday movements.

Think of each session, each movement, and each repetition as practice rather than an all out race to the finish line. The race can and will come later, but right now in the beginning, your task is to slowly get the body accustomed to these new movements.

You'll have plenty of time to let the arrow fly once your body is ready.

WE'RE NOT DOING THE SAME THINGS ON ANY GIVEN DAY, HOW DOES ANYONE GET BETTER?

Remember the entire purpose here is this:

> *"CONSTANTLY VARIED FUNCTIONAL MOVEMENTS EXECUTED AT HIGH INTENSITY ACROSS BROAD TIME AND MODAL DOMAINS," WITH THE STATED GOAL OF IMPROVING FITNESS, WHICH IT DEFINES AS "WORK CAPACITY ACROSS BROAD TIME AND MODAL DOMAINS."*

The whole point is to get the body accustomed to being able to do a variety of different things, at a variety of intensities, with the goal of improving fitness overall. The really magical thing about performing so many different tasks in a given week, is the ability to see what specific things you are prone to enjoy the most. One can then take these findings and tweak them as the journey unfolds such as signing up for an obstacle race, joining an Olympic lifting team, joining a powerlifting team, or running a distance race. Then, as you discover the things you may not enjoy as much, you'll soon know the feelings of accomplishment and power that come hand in hand with mastering something truly difficult. It's an addictive feeling, and there is no shortage of opportunities here. Embrace them.

There are a few things I learned through trial and error over the last several years of the journey, and it was hard not to include them when compiling this book. I say this because I know everyone who begins anything new (not just a path within fitness) will likely encounter some or all of these points as they go. Here are some thoughts to reflect on when starting anything for the first time, and may be useful to come back to later on.

Do you first.

You'll have a lot to take in during the first few months and sometimes longer, so don't get too caught up in the details - just put in the consistent work. Eventually as you progress, you'll find certain people whom you may look to as role models or for support, but in the beginning it will be tough to discern one person from the next based on a few moments of observation.

Instead, pay attention to the important things, namely how your body is feeling, and how you can perfect the movements yourself, because you're not going to know if the others you see online or in gyms are doing the movements correctly anyway.

Make a point to focus on counting your repetitions accurately, because you'll find that the ability to keep track in your head may be fleeting during a set of 100 jumps over a rope or 30 burpees. It's easy to get lazy with your counting and revert to finishing up when it 'feels like you're done.' Do not short yourself here, and complete the work as prescribed, without shortcuts.

Track your progress

Record your numbers, your times, your weights for various lifts, and major accomplishments like your first real push-up or set of 50 burpees. Bring a notebook with you if you need, or start by using the lined section in the back of the printed version of this book. I encourage you to jot down the times and numbers as you are starting, so that you can track your progress as you go along. This is a highly powerful exercise in itself, to be able to look back at a former best lift, and beat it. You'll find it empowering to know that you did a certain number of push-ups last month, and record many more the next time. For this reason, I've included additional space within the pages of this book, so that you may have one centralized place to note these items as you achieve them.

If using heavy equipment, this is an extremely vital area in which to pay attention: Where you're letting the equipment fall, and where your focus is when the bar or anything else is over your head.

In other words:

1. Don't let anything drop to the deck without stepping out of the way.

2. When doing any overhead movement, whether it be with the bar, kettlebell, or dumbell, pay attention to where these pieces of equipment are at all times.

3. If the movement requires you to fix your gaze on something other than said piece of equipment, for the sake of all that is right in the world, please keep your focus on the location of that equipment.

4. More often than not, you're going to have a heavy piece of iron over your head. You want to know where it is at all times, period.

"They" are not watching you –

Remember, if you are training at a gym, everyone else *should* be working too hard and sweating too much to pay attention to what anyone else is doing (unless of course it's a high five and congratulations on completing a tough workout). Despite thinking they might be watching you like hawks, they're not. Not even a little bit. If they are, they're missing the whole point of training and you shouldn't care what they think simply because of this.

Even with all of this said, you'll still experience the paranoia of Strongman Sven staring you down while you complete your fifth set of 30 burpees, but you'll soon realize that you don't even hear what music is playing when you're in the middle of a tough set of work like that. So, rest assured that the last thing you'll remember is what the person next to you was doing, and you can be certain they won't remember the details of what you did either (unless it is a celebratory high five for a job well done at the end of course).

There are many things to learn here, so to keep from being overwhelmed, try to find the movements and lifts you enjoy the most, and that you are naturally good at. Some people are fantastic at the dead lift out of the gate but are slower on the rowing machine, while others may be extremely fast runners but yet might have a harder time moving the big weights off the floor. People with shorter limbs and torsos might blow the pants off of the taller folks in their speed for burpees and ability to move heavy weights overhead, while the taller individuals may find it way more efficient to row a fast 800 meter or jump the first leg of a rope climb almost half way up from the start. Of course, there is no actual way to categorize what a given person will be good at or need to work harder to improve on, but these points are meant to get you thinking in terms of how you might use what you've got to your advantage once you get a feel for what works easily, and what might need extra attention.

In the beginning it is especially helpful to give yourself a mental boost by putting a LOT of positive thought towards the things you gravitate to, and then working on the rest with increased intensity as you get better. The nice thing about these workouts, is that you'll always be required to do the things that you dislike at one point or another, so there's no escaping those things anyway and you may as well be thankful for when something you are good at is scrawled across the page for that day!

OBSERVING OTHER PEOPLE AT THE GYM OR ONLINE –

When you start getting into the groove of things, you're probably going to pinpoint those who are extremely good at every. Thing. Once you're feeling like you have some footing, try to see these beasts as examples to strive towards, rather than letting it get you down for not keeping up. They were new once too, they get it! Furthermore, you'll start noticing that newer people will come along who are similar to where you were when you started. Try to help give them a positive and encouraging experience by greeting them by name when they come in, cheering them on, helping them out if it looks like they might need a high five, or even finishing up the end of a workout with them if you've completed it sooner and they are the last ones.

These little things can have a huge impact on a new member's experience and for the gym as a whole. I believe that if each person makes an effort to smile and be an overall positive influence, the more people we will have to champion the integrity of our fitness community.

You got this.

Pick a number, put it in your head, and stick with it. - Whether it's setting the clock for 5AM and forcing yourself to open your eyes to get out of bed rather than hitting snooze, setting a number of 5 days per week to hit up the gym, setting a number of 20 wall balls before setting the medicine ball down, or pushing through an 800 meter row before slowing down.

Put a number in your head, and stick to it. Let that number resonate in your mind when the muscles are aching and the lungs are hurting. You'll thank yourself next time the same exercise comes across your plate, because you'll know that you've already done it and can do it again.

Remember, consistency over the long term will result in continual improvement.

For crying out loud Have fun!

This isn't a contest to the death. No one is going to knock you down and steal your shoes if you trip up on your jump rope for the tenth time today. The best part about working together with people who are in the middle of the same struggles as you is that you can glance over at your neighbor, cheer them on, and smile when it's done knowing you did more work in one hour than 99% of the population does in a week.

GLOSSARY OF TERMS

You may be wondering about the various types of movements listed out in the *Original Sessions*. Since this list is far shorter than the variety of movements you are performing in the *Home Editions* I've outlined them at a glance here.

AMRAP: A workout type that stands for "as many rounds as possible" in a given amount of time. For example, count the number of push-ups you can do in 5 minutes. One might see "AMRAP 10 (5 push-ups, 5 pull-ups). In this case one would keep track of how many sets of 5 push-ups and 5 pull-ups completed during 10 minutes.

Assault bike: A variation on the stationary bike, this little devil of a chariot on wheels packs a huge metabolic hit while recruiting the arms and legs to push, pull, and pedal one's way to nowhere. Typical units of measurement are distance and calories burned. Tip for the assault bike: If the legs start burning, compensate by pushing heavier with your arms. If the arms start to give out, help them out by pedaling harder with the legs for a little while. The beauty about this beast is the ability to adjust where your power is coming from. Just remember, "Arms and legs, arms and legs, arms and legs . . ."

Barbell: The glistening, sometimes rusty metal rod of glory on which bumper plates are placed for lifting. This staple will become your best friend, mortal enemy, and invaluable mentor in the days and years to come. Treat it with respect, but know that if you absolutely must curse at it, that is completely acceptable to do so. Just remember to say you're sorry afterward. Weight of the barbell for men is 20 kilograms (44 pounds) and 15 kilograms (33 pounds) for women.

Below parallel: This is a position in the squat movement where the hip crease ends up below the knees. Not everyone will have the mobility to squat this low to the deck. Your coach will be able to work with you to find what best suits your anatomy in the squat movements.

Box Jump: A jump from the ground onto a regular old (yet very stable) wooden box, or any other elevated surface. Pay attention to what you are doing on this one, as it is quite common to catch a toe or otherwise end up with missing skin from the shins as a result of a fall. This movement is typically performed onto a 20-inch or 24-inch box, however can be performed at any height. Anyone who may be unfamiliar with a higher jump can easily start with just a few inches off the ground by using a bumper plate, and working their way up. Literally. Some gyms may have a softer version of the wooden box for those learning as well. These are usually made of a foam interior, and are fantastic on the joints for a softer landing, and of course, easing into the movement without as much risk of a shin skin grabber.

Bumper plates: Round, virtually indestructible donuts of mighty capacity, these are weights that are used for placing on a barbell. They are made of materials that are a bit softer (instead of plain metal) so that when dropping they are not as hard on the surface flooring. You'll notice many different use cases for these off the bar as well. Plates can be carried overhead for distance, grasped between the fingers to train grip strength, placed overhead for adding weight to a sit- up, or even chained around the waist for added resistance in pull-ups.

Burpee: Your go-to, all body, no equipment required tool in the box. This is a series of movements starting with the standing position. Squat down, place the hands on the floor on either side of the feet, move the legs back into a push up position, move legs back up into a squatting position, stand, and finally jump up to an overhead clapping of the hands. Legs can either walk back into and out of the pushup position, or can jump back. Depending on a person's tolerance for impact, this one can easily be scaled by using the walk back method, and will still be a very effective way to increase the heart rate and engage all muscles of the body. When traveling, do a set of 200 in the mornings from your hotel room, or hit the deck in the airport and knock out as many as you can while waiting for your next connection. When you're unable to make it to the gym, the burpee will not disappoint in terms of getting a full body workout in a short amount of time. You've got your squats and push-ups covered, along with the huge metabolic hit that comes along with quickly getting down to the ground and back up again repeatedly.

Butterfly pull-up: Watching someone execute this movement well is quite awe inspiring. This is a variation of the pull-ups, and gets its name from how similar it is to the butterfly swimming technique, only while hanging from a pull-ups bar. It is mainly used when the goal is to get through a long set of pull-ups quickly. Once mastered, it is an extremely efficient way to utilize the force of the hips to move the body upward for many repetitions. Due to the high workload placed on the hands, it is recommended to work up to this slowly rather than risk tearing.

Butterfly sit-up: A nice variation on the classic crunch. This movement starts in the seated position with the feet together and knees splayed outward towards the floor. Lay back to the floor behind you, move arms overhead to touch the floor overhead, and then sit back up, leaning back over the feet. Add a bumper plate or kettlebell for added resistance.

Captain Whiteboard: The board on which the WOD (workout of the day) is written for all to follow during the course of the next hour or so. Rather than barking orders, this guy silently instructs via dry erase marker fumes. It is just as effective, I might add.

Chipper: A workout type that requires for all repetitions of a movement to be done before moving to the next movement. An example might be: 50 air squats, 40 sit ups, 30 walking lunges, 20 push-ups, 10 pull-ups. Working/chipping away at the movements until completion is the name of the game. The good news is, once you finish with one movement you won't have to do it again (usually)!

Clean: A barbell lift that starts with the bar on the ground, and ends resting on the shoulders at the front of the neck. The bar movement is straight up the belly, keeping the hips low at first. There are many small details to this movement that can take a very long time to master, so do not get discouraged with this one!

Clean and jerk: One of two Olympic lifts, the other being the Snatch. This is a barbell movement with many small nuances, but in short it is taking the bar from the ground to the shoulders, and then powerfully moving it upwards above the head to lockout.

Deadlift: One of several power lifts involving the barbell. With many finer points to be discovered by each individual person, this one at the root level is raising the barbell from the ground up to the hips and setting it back down. There are entire books written about this movement alone, so do not let the simplicity illustrated here full you. Envision the arms as ropes and the hands as vices gripping the bar ferociously as you stand up with it. This is not a 'pull' from the ground. It is standing up forcefully while not letting the bar go.

Dislocates: Excellent shoulder mobility drill, commonly used as part of a warm up. With a narrow PVC pipe (about a meter or so long) hold in a wide grip and pass from hips back over head and end at your butt.

Double Under: Jumping rope with a bit more wrist action. This movement requires for the jump rope to make two passes under the feet with each jump upward.

EMOM: A workout type that stands for "every minute on the minute." This simply means one would complete a designated amount of repetitions each minute. Using our trusty push-ups and pull ups combination, an example might be "EMOM 10 (5 pus-hups, 5 pull-ups). When the clock starts, one would complete 5 push-ups and 5 pull-ups, and rest for the remainder of the minute until the next minute starts. Wash, rinse, repeat for 10 minutes.

GHD machine: (glute ham developer) In many gyms this underused piece of equipment sits off on the sidelines. In fact, it is a wonderful way to strengthen the hamstrings, glutes, abs, and back, and aids in preventing hamstring strains and back injuries. Some of the common exercises done on this machine are: the hip and back extension, glute ham raise, and sit up. Hug a bumper plate close to your chest to add more resistance to your efforts on this one, and watch your core strength soar.

Handstand push-up: This is exactly how it sounds. A dizzying upside down shoulder roaster, it is performed against a wall for balance. One starts in a handstand position and then lowers the head to the floor, and then pushes back up.

Hang: A barbell position where one stands with the barbell 'hanging' by the hands. A use case for the hang would be a variation of the Clean. Instead of starting with the barbell on the ground, one starts at the hang position, takes a slight dip downwards, and moves the barbell up to the shoulders at the front of the neck to finish.

Hero WODs: (workout of the day) These workouts are tributes to a fallen first responders or members of the military. You might see a workout around Memorial Day for example, called "Murph." This one takes about an hour or less for people to complete and consists of a 1 mile run, 100 pull-ups, 200 push-ups, 300 air squats, and a 1 mile run to top it off. All while wearing a 20 pound weighted vest as if the work wasn't enough. Don't let it intimate you though. This is a phenomenal chance to test your progress annually by recording your time and trying to beat it next year.

Hopper: A workout type that is put together by sheer luck of the draw, such as using a deck of cards. An example might be: clubs = push-ups, diamonds = pull-ups, spades = air squats, hearts = burpees. If a 5 of hearts is drawn, everyone does 5 burpees. One might be surprised and perhaps horrified at the sheer amount of work involved in a 52 card deck of playing cards. No need to fear though, it'll all be over in an hour.

Kettlebell: A round piece of steel with a handle. Lovingly referred to as "cannon balls with handles" these minimalist pieces of equipment are a staple in many gyms, with an unlimited potential for variety. Typical movements with the kettlebell are: swings, snatches, cleans, squats, presses, and Turkish get-ups. There are entire certifications that athletes can acquire for kettlebells alone, so if you find yourself falling in love with these cold spheres of iron, you might want to research their full potential and find out what they are capable of with the right knowhow.

Kettlebell swing (American style): Kettlebell ends up overhead. Using one kettlebell with both hands, picture the movement required to hike a football back between the legs, followed by an explosive hip thrust to propel the bell forward and overhead, rather than stopping at eye level as with the traditional Russian style swing.

Kettlebell swing (Russian style): Kettlebell ends up at eye level. Using one kettlebell with both hands, picture the movement required to hike a football back between the legs, followed by an explosive hip thrust to propel the bell forward to eye level, rather than overhead as with the American style swing. For this reason, one can also add variety to the Russian swing by performing the above with one hand, switch between hands, or use double kettlebells. All of these movements have an astounding effect on the full body, firing up the hamstrings, glutes, abdominals, and shoulders. Typical prescribed weights for men are 53 pounds, and 35 pounds for women. This is base level, and most gyms will have a full range of kettlebells from 18 pounds going up to the 108 pound beast. Bells were originally measured in poods (one mood = 36 pounds) but you'll see them measured in pounds and kilograms these days.

Kipping pull-ups: A variation on the pull-ups, deriving from a combination of a 'kick' and a 'pull-ups.' A fairly technical move to master, this form of pull-ups allows for many repetitions to be completed in a short amount of time. This movement utilizes momentum from the hips to move the body up to the pull-ups bar while relying on the shoulders to hinge open and closed to complete the series. Because it relies more on the full body movement to be faster and more efficient, it is sometimes frowned upon by those who are hard core strict pull-ups practitioners.

Metcon: A workout term that is short for "metabolic conditioning." These types of workouts switch between cardio and strength. An example might be 20 deadlifts followed by a 200 meter run, repeated several times.

Muscle-up: A literal step up from the classic pull-ups, this movement requires more of a gymnastic approach and is typically performed on a set of rings (this can also be done on a pull-ups bar, referred to as a bar muscle-up). To complete this movement, one grips a set of rings overhead and pulls the body up forcefully, ending with the arms extended and rings at hip level. A complex movement that for most, requires many hours of practice. Do not fear though, there are many ways to scale this one.

Olympic lifts: Two lifts performed in the Olympics and other Olympic lifting meets, the Snatch and the Clean and Jerk.

Overhead Squat: With the barbell overhead and arms locked out in a wide grip, this is a lowering of the body by sitting the hips back as if to sit down into a chair, and lowering down towards the ground before rising back up.

Parallettes: Small bars that sit off the ground around 8 inches which are used for movements such as L-sits (legs outstretched in front of the body while the arms hold the body up a few inches off the ground) or for placing against the wall to allow for handstand push-ups to be more difficult (if there is such a thing!).

Pistol: A variation on the squat movement, done on one leg. From the side, the body looks like a pistol when in the bottom position because the leg not in use is outstretched to the front, while the working leg is bending close to the body. These movements can be done with bodyweight only, or weighted with a dumbbell, plate, or kettlebell to increase difficulty. This one is easily modified by placing a box close to the body to sit back onto, rather than having to lower all the way to the ground and back up.

Power Clean: A barbell lift that involves raising the bar from the floor to the shoulders in front of the neck, while landing in a partial squat instead of a full squat.

PR: Personal record. It can be extremely gratifying to start writing down your workouts on a calendar or in a notebook when you begin your journey. You can then look back at where you started, and compare how far you've come. For this reason, I've left bonus space within the pages of this book in case you would like to record some of these numbers here.

Prowler: Also referred to as a sled. These metal contraptions with handles are loaded with weight plates and pushed across the ground for a set distance, turned around, and pushed back. The wind is taken out of the sails quickly with a heavy sled push, as it requires much output from the larger muscle groups of the quads.

Rig: A term used to refer to the overall steel structures that support barbells for lifting and pull-ups bars.

Rope climb: Climbing up a rope and back down. These can be done using arms only, or practiced with the legs clamped around the rope to help propel one upward. There are many scaling options for these so do not worry or let this one intimidate you; you'll get there!

Rower: Most all CrossFit gyms have rowing machines. A fantastic way to recruit all muscle groups and obtain a no-impact high metabolic hit. Typical units of measurement are distance, wattage/output, and calories. If running is too hard on your joints, or if an injury is nagging at you, the rower can be used in place of running until the body is ready for more impact

Rx'd: Short for "as prescribed" as in, doing the workout at the recommended weights without scaling back or modifying.

Sandbags: Ranging from 10-70 pounds typically, sandbags are a great addition to running. Some workouts may incorporate the sandbag for squats, shoulder toss overs, and various barbell movement replacements to train grip and handling of oddly shaped objects.

Scaled: The ability (and in most cases, the recommendation) to modify any workout to fit the needs of each individual. This could mean jumping pull-ups instead of strict knees on the floor push-ups, lowering the weight for lifts, stepping up onto a box instead of box jumps or rowing instead of running. Most every athlete with the exception of the elites will scale in one way or another, so you will be in good company when your coach instructs you to scale as well.

Ski erg: This is a piece of equipment that is best described as a vertical rowing machine. The mechanics are similar, however instead of sitting down and going through a rowing motion, one stands up and pulls the handles from overhead to the floor, as if downhill skiing. Measurements are typically distance, watts, or calories.

Snatch: One of two Olympic lifts, the other being the Clean and Jerk. The barbell is pulled from the ground with a very wide grip, and quickly turned overhead in one movement while landing in a partial or full squat. The movement ends when the body and arms are at a full lockout overhead. This is a highly technical, if not the most technical lift you'll do, so take the time to learn and practice it well.

Strict pull-ups: Pulling the body upward to the bar starting at a complete hang, with no kipping movement to assist. Once the neck is level with the bar, the body is then lowered back down to a dead hang. pull-ups can be scaled in many different ways, so do not be discouraged if this is a no go at first. One may begin by placing a box or series of bumper plates beneath the bar, and jumping the body up to neck level with the bar. When a long set of these becomes doable, one might transition to a banded pull-up. Many gyms have bands of various thicknesses available for use in a variety of different ways, and this is a great way to help develop strength in pull-ups. The idea is to take weight off the body by placing the foot or knee in the loop of a band that has been wrapped onto the top of the pull-ups bar. When performing the movement, the resistance of the band works like a person giving you a literal hand up to the bar. As your strength builds, you can decrease the size and resistance of the band, until you no longer need one at all to perform the movement.

Squat clean: A barbell lift that starts with the bar on the ground, and ends resting on the shoulders at the front of the neck with legs in a full squat position. The lift ends with standing up to full body lockout.

Tabata: A fast workout type consisting of 20 seconds of all out work (to the point of not being able to talk to your neighbor) followed by a 10 second "rest" which never seems to last long enough before going into the next 20 seconds of work. This sequence is repeated 8 times totaling 4 minutes of work. The magic of this beauty comes with the intensity with which the athlete performs during the 20 seconds of work. Those 20 seconds are meant to be utilized as an all out, full capacity block of work during which one should not be able to muster up the ability to form words.

Thruster: Once referred to as the devil's asshole, this barbell movement begins in a full squat with the barbell resting at the shoulders in front of the neck, with elbows pointed to the sky as much as possible. One then rises to standing while pressing the bar overhead in one solid movement. Wash, rinse, repeat for a set of 10 and you'll soon understand the nickname.

Tires: Good old farm equipment tires have been a staple at many gyms, mainly used for rolling, flipping, or slamming with sledgehammers. A good, wholesome way to take out any aggression or stress from a hard day at the office, these things won't complain or mope or backtalk, no matter what you do to them.

Toes to Bar: Starting at a hang from the pull-ups bar, the toes are raised to tough the bar between the hands. Scaling options for this movement include: raising just the knees as high up as possible, or lying on the ground perpendicular to the rig with hands holding onto the rig overhead.and raising the legs up to touch the rig.

Turkish get-up: An all body movement typically performed with a kettlebell. Simply put, with the kettlebell locked out overhead, the practitioner will get down onto the ground, onto their back and back up again, or vice versa by starting on the floor first and going through the same sequence. The finer details take some getting used to, but if we were to break it down into a few steps they would be: Start on your back, with a kettlebell in your right arm held locked out above your head. Do not take your eyes off the bell. Bend the same knee as the arm holding the bell. Thrust your core upward, so that you are propped up on the opposite forearm (in this case, the left forearm). Shoot the hips up, so that the body is in a plank, and then get yourself onto your left hand as your left arm is supporting the weight. The left (non-bent) leg then swings behind you like a windshield wiper, positioning itself so that the body may rise up into a lungess with the right leg in front and left leg behind. Come to full standing with both legs straight. Step back with the left leg and do the entire process in reverse. This is a good one to observe as a seasoned practitioner performs the movement, so that you can get a good visual before practicing on your own. A great way to practice is to use a shoe or something light in place of the kettlebell to get a feel for the sequence before placing a ball of iron overhead.

Wall ball: A medicine ball ranging in weight from 6 to 30 pounds (usual weights for women are 14 pounds, 20 pounds for men) which is thrown overhead against a wall to hit a target 9-10 feet high). The ball is then caught in a full squat before being launched upward again, repeatedly for the duration of the workout or prescribed number of repetitions.

WOD: Workout of the day. As soon as you arrive at the gym, your eyes will gravitate over to the ever present oracle of a whiteboard, on which the WOD will be inscribed. Some gyms may have the WOD projected for all to see on a fancy flat screen, however most places will still use ye olde Captain Whiteboard for simplicity sake.

ABOUT THE AUTHOR

Residing in Montana, the author holds the elite certification as a Strong First Kettlebell Instructor (SFG1). In addition, she regularly coaches as a Crossfit Level 1 Trainer (CF-L1). Over the last 20 years, Heidi has deeply researched and extensively experimented with various health and fitness protocols, and is now working to combine what she has learned in these arenas with her colorful roots as a self made author in order to share as much as possible.

NOTES

CPSIA information can be obtained
at www.ICGtesting.com
Printed in the USA
BVHW011023181120
593415BV00023B/901

9 781087 924717